Chambers' Guide To London The Secret City

Chambers' Guide
to
London
The Secret City

Michael Chambers

◢ millington

First published in Great Britain in 1974 by
Ocean Books Ltd. This edition published in
1979 by
Millington Books
an imprint of
Davison Publishing Ltd
109 Southampton Row
London WC1B 4HH

Typeset by Computacomp (UK) Ltd
Fort William, Scotland
Printed by Tonbridge Printers, Tonbridge, Kent

Contents

Murderers' London

Jack the Ripper, Christie, Seddon, Crippen—names to send a shiver down the spine. Yet there is something strangely fascinating about famous murders and the places they were committed.

7

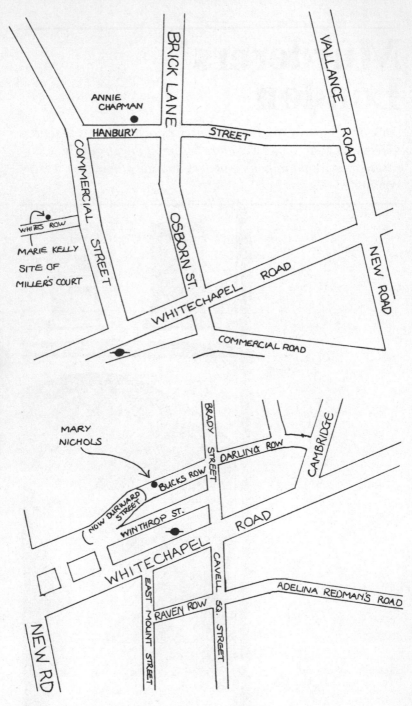

The Unsolved Mystery of Jack the Ripper
Whitechapel, E1

Who was 'Jack the Ripper', the vicious murderer whose gruesome crimes have roused the morbid curiosity of several generations? Theories about his identity abound. It has even been suggested that the police knew who he was but suppressed the evidence because it pointed to a member of the aristocracy, even worse—to a member of the Royal Family.

In the Autumn of 1888 Jack the Ripper carried out a series of murders, each more dreadful than the one before, that terrorised the East End and caused a national outcry verging on hysteria. His first victim was Mary Nichols, who was found in Buck's Row (now Durward Street), Whitechapel, late at night on Friday 31st August with her throat cut. The injuries were terrible. Her head was nearly severed from her body and two large gashes ripped her open from the lower abdomen to her breast. Like the other victims she was a prostitute in her 40's. In a letter to a Fleet Street news agency Jack the Ripper wrote 'I am down on whores and I shan't quit ripping them till I do get buckled'.

The second victim was Annie Chapman, aged 47, also a prostitute, whose body was found in the backyard of 29 Hanbury Street on Friday night, 7th September. The occupants of this little slum house discovered her corpse with its neck cut through to the spine and the body slashed open. Her uterus had been removed and her intestines lifted out and placed over her shoulder. The uterus was never found.

In the early hours of Sunday morning, 30th September, the body of yet another prostitute, Elizabeth Stride, aged 45, a Swedish woman known as Long Liz, was found in the yard of 40 Berner Street (now Henriques Street) off Commercial Road. She had only just been killed: the body was warm and the blood still oozing from a gash in her throat. There was no other mutilation and it was assumed

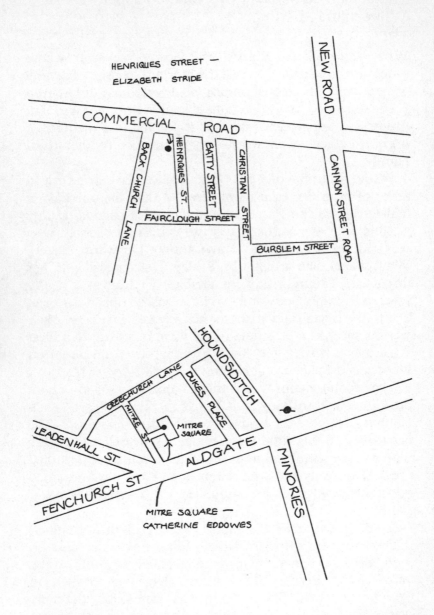

HENRIQUES STREET —
ELIZABETH STRIDE

NEW ROAD

COMMERCIAL ROAD

BACK CHURCH LANE

HENRIQUES ST.

BATTY STREET

CHRISTIAN STREET

CANNON STREET ROAD

FAIRCLOUGH STREET

BURSLEM STREET

HOUNDSDITCH

CREECHURCH LANE

MITRE ST.

DUKES PLACE

MITRE SQUARE

LEADENHALL ST

ALDGATE

MINORIES

FENCHURCH ST

MITRE SQUARE —
CATHERINE EDDOWES

Jack the Ripper had been interrupted before he could complete his butchery. Denied his usual satisfaction, the Ripper went on to kill his fourth victim later that same night. She was Catherine Eddowes, aged 43, who was found with her throat slashed in the south west corner of Mitre Square, Aldgate. The body of this poor woman had been mutilated almost beyond recognition. Her face was disfigured, part of her right ear cut off, her abdomen ripped open and her entrails turned out and flung in a heap about her neck. The kidney and ovaries were also removed and were never found.

The police were intrigued by the boldness and daring of the murderer. After all, Mitre Court was patrolled by a policeman every 15 minutes and people were constantly milling around. They were also intrigued by his skill with the knife and his apparent knowledge of anatomy. In all cases the victim had been silenced immediately by a precise incision through the vocal chords. And the long incisions in the abdomen together with the removal of various organs suggested some experience in surgery. This led to a popular belief (at a time of Jewish immigration and of growing anti-semitism) that Jack the Ripper was a Jewish schochet or ritual slaughterer.

With each successive butchery, the murderer's appetite for blood and mutilation increased. His last victim suffered the most dreadul ripping of all. Marie Kelly, an attractive young girl of 25, was found on Friday November 9th lying naked on her bed at 13 Miller's Court off Dorset Street (now Whites Row) near Commercial Street. Like the other victims she was a prostitute, but was the only one to be attacked in her own home. Her throat had been slit in the usual fashion, her ears and nose cut off, and her breasts removed and placed on a small bedside table along with her heart and kidneys. Her abdomen had been cut open and her liver placed on her right thigh. Yet again the uterus had been removed and was never found. This was the Ripper's last crime, the culminating horror that may at last have satisfied his hideous appetite for blood.

No satisfactory identification of the Ripper has ever been made. The author's theory is that Jack the Ripper was a woman and that she was known to the victims she killed. This would explain why she was never detected and why the local prostitutes, who were very much on their guard at the time, allowed her to accompany them alone in deserted back streets and dark squares. She was probably in her 50's, a retired prostitute, perhaps, who continued to earn money as an abortionist serving the community of prostitutes in and around Spitalfields (where all the victims lived). It is well known among those at Scotland Yard who specialise in such matters that many backstreet abortionists are women in their 50's or 60's, usually childless and often ex-prostitutes, who do the job partly for the money but also for the curious satisfaction it gives them. The Ripper needed no strength, merely an unsuspecting victim, since the throat was slashed from behind. In the case of Marie Kelly, who was murdered in her own bed, the Ripper had probably been invited in to give her an abortion. That she was pregnant was not discovered because her uterus had been removed. But it is interesting that she was the only victim who could have been pregnant at the time of her death, the others all being well over 40, and she was the only one to die in her own bed. This theory explains why the victim was never 'sexually assaulted'. It also explains the Ripper's bizarre obsession with the victim's uterus.

The spot where Catherine Eddowes body was found in Mitre Square is still known as 'Ripper's Corner'. It is said that Catherine's ghost can be seen here when the square is deserted, huddling against the wall near the iron stairs of a fire-escape in the early hours of the morning.

The Kray Twins
Bethnal Green
East End Mafia

During the 1960's London's underworld was dominated by two powerful gangs: the Kray twins in Bethnal Green and the Richardson Brothers in Bermondsey. The gangs would run protection rackets milking the illegal profits of West End gambling clubs. The police knew what was going on but lacked sufficient evidence to prosecute. Witnesses were too scared to talk.

Reginald and Ronald Kray are identical twins, born in 1933 at 64 Stean Street, Hoxton. For most of their childhood they lived in Bethnal Green at 178 Vallance Road. In their teens they took up boxing and after a few years in the British Army, chose a career of crime. Having served their apprenticeship under Billy Hill, they set up their own firm in 1959 and made a name for themselves as vicious and unmerciful thugs. They enjoyed being seen in West End clubs and being photographed in the company of famous celebrities.

There was continual gang rivalry between the Krays and the Richardsons which reached a climax when the Richardson Brothers were arrested in 1966, leaving George Cornell as head of their gang. Ronnie decided that now was the time to liquidate his rivals once and for all by killing Cornell. Ronnie took his 9-mm Mauser Automatic and asked one of his thugs to drive him to *The Blind Beggar*, a pub in Whitechapel Road where he had heard his intended victim was drinking. When he arrived he found the pub almost empty save for a couple near the door and an old man on the other side of the partition. The barmaid was putting a record on the juke box and Cornell was sitting on a stool at the far end of the bar. Cornell had been the Richardsons' strong-arm man and had a reputation as the toughest member of the gang. When Ronnie entered he

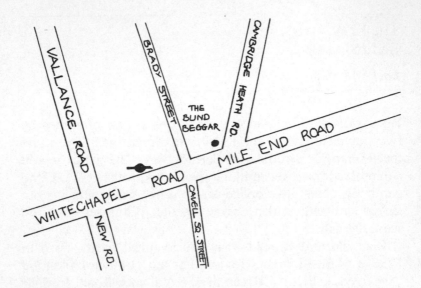

smiled and said: 'Well, just look who's here'. Ronnie walked up to him, drew his automatic, and shot him point blank through the head.

Soon everyone in the East End knew of the murder and who had done it, but none of the witnesses would talk. This reckless public killing made Ronnie Kray the most feared gangster in the country, and it was to be two years before the police were able to build up their case against him.

The Krays began to indulge in violence on an ever-increasing scale. Ronnie would boast of his killing and urge his brother to kill someone as he had done. Eventually Reggie agreed to kill Jack McVitie, a smalltime East End crook who had been unwise enough to provoke the Krays.

On the pretence that he was invited to a party McVitie was induced to turn up alone at a basement flat in Cazenove Road, Stoke Newington, where the Krays and their heavies were waiting for him. 'Where's all the birds, where's the booze?' shouted McVitie as he burst into the room. Reggie pulled out his gun, aimed it at his head and pulled the trigger, but the gun jammed. Bedlam then ensued. They all jumped on McVitie who in a desperate effort to break free threw himself through the window. He got stuck, however, and was pulled back into the room by his legs. Ronnie then held him with his hands behind his back facing Reggie. 'Kill him, Reg. Do him', shouted Ron. 'Don't stop now'. Reggie raised his butcher's knife and plunged it into McVitie's face below the eye. McVitie collapsed on the floor while Reggie continued to stab him in the stomach and chest, finally impaling him on the floor with the knife stuck through his throat. The body was then disposed of, never to be found again, and the blood-stained flat thoroughly cleaned.

A special gang-busters squad was formed at Scotland Yard to tackle the Krays and after much painstaking work achieved a breakthrough. The barmaid at The Blind Beggar who had witnessed the shooting of Cornell, and an accomplice of the Krays at Cazenove Road were persuaded to give evidence for the prosecution. As a result, the Kray twins were arrested in May 1968, found guilty of murder and sentenced to life imprisonment.

John Christie
Ruston Close, W11

Bodies under the floorboards

On 24th March, 1953, a tenant of No. 10 Rillington Place, was attempting to fix a shelf against the kitchen wall for his wireless set. To his surprise the wall came away to reveal a hidden recess, and by the light of his torch he saw the corpse of a woman, later identified as Hectorina Maclennan. He called the police who searched the house and unearthed one body after another. A warrant was issued immediately for the arrest of the previous tenant, John Christie, who had disappeared.

Christie was born of respectable parents in Yorkshire. In 1902 he married Ethel. They never had any children and he

15

is said to have been impotent. She left him several times, but from 1938 they lived together at Rillington Place, North Kensington. The house had no bathroom and the only lavatory was in a shed in the backyard.

During the War while serving as a Special Constable attached to Harrow Road police station he murdered Ruth Fuerst, a 17 year old student nurse who went home with him one night while his wife was away on holiday. In Christie's own words: 'While I was having intercourse with her, I strangled her with a piece of rope. I took her from the bedroom into the front room and put her under the floorboards. I had to do that because of my wife coming back. I put the remainder of her clothes under the floorboards too'. Subsequently he dug a hole in the garden where he buried the body. 'After it was over I never gave it a thought'.

On leaving the police force in 1943 Christie worked for an electrical firm where he met Muriel Eady. She complained of bronchial catarrh and Christie assured her he could cure this ailment if she would try some of his Friar's Balsam. She called on him while his wife was out and he produced a piece of rubber tubing from which she was to breath the beneficial fumes. The tube, however, was connected to the gas fire and the unwary Muriel fell unconscious. He then carried her across to his bedroom. 'I had intercourse with her and strangled her'. Again he disposed of the body in the garden, where he subsequently grew runner beans.

In 1948 Timothy Evans and his wife Beryl moved into 10 Rillington Place, occupying the top flat above the Christies. Beryl Evans was already pregnant and in October she gave birth to a daughter. She soon became pregnant again but it was so cramped in their tiny flat that she decided to have an abortion. Her husband was against the idea. Christie, however, who had become quite friendly with them, offered to help. After Evans had gone out to work he went up to Beryl, forced her to have sexual intercourse with him and in the excitement strangled her.

Evans, who was mentally retarded and illiterate, was

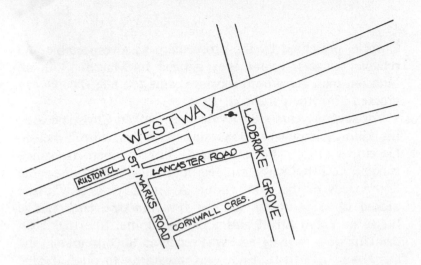

persuaded by Christie that his wife had died during an abortion and since they were both implicated he would have to help him dispose of the body. They carried it downstairs into an empty room and Christie told Evans he would later put the body in a drain outside the front of the house. He also told Evans he knew of a young couple who would be prepared to adopt his baby and asked him to dress her so that she could be taken away. The following day while Evans was at work Christie strangled the baby with a tie. He then removed the bodies of the mother and child and hid them under the floor of the wash house. When Evans returned he was told that the young couple had collected the child and that he should sell his belongings and leave town.

Evans went to stay with relatives at Merthyr Vale who kept asking him about his family. After a few weeks he confessed to being involved in the disappearance of his wife, and told the police that her body was in a drain in front of 10 Rillington Place. The drain was searched and was found to be empty, but her corpse was eventually discovered with the dead baby in the wash house. The police questioned their old colleague, Christie, and were satisfied that the murderer was Timothy Evans. They took poor Evans to Notting Hill police station and interrogated him with the usual courtesies. After some time he confessed, although at the trial he maintained his innocence. Chief witness for the prosecution was

Christie, presented by the prosecution as a respectable and reliable witness. Evans was hanged in March 1950, an innocent man for whom reprieve came too late. The Queen granted him free pardon in 1966.

For several years after Evans was hanged Christie ceased his killing. However, beginning with his wife Ethel in December 1952, he murdered four women in quick succession. Ethel was strangled in bed and buried under the floorboards of the front room. A few days later Christie picked up a prostitute in *The Westminister Arms* public house in Praed Street and took her home. She had been drinking quite heavily and was rendered unconscious in the same way as Muriel Eady—by breathing through a tube connected to the gasfire. Christie then strangled her with a rope during sexual intercourse. Her body was hidden in a recess in the kitchen behind a cupboard and covered over with ashes. He did exactly the same to another prostitute, Rita Nelson, a few days later and she too ended up behind the kitchen cupboard.

His last victim was a 26-year-old girl called Hectorina Maclennan. She put up a brave struggle when Christie tried to gas her but was strangled all the same, and joined the other two corpses in the kitchen. Christie then disappeared and tramped about the London streets sleeping rough. On the 24th March the bodies were discovered, and on the 31st March Christie was seen by a police constable on the Embankment near Putney Bridge. He gave his name as 'John Waddington' but was recognised and taken to Putney police station. At his trial in June he was found guilty, and was hanged on the 15th July 1953.

Rillington Place is now called Ruston Close, but the house at number 10 has been demolished. An exact copy of the kitchen where the bodies were hidden was made at the time of Christie's trial and can still be seen in the Chamber of Horrors at *Madame Tussaud's*. The steeple of the derelict church in Rillington Place is clearly visible to the left of the A 40 motorway as you drive west, just before reaching the Shepherd's Bush exit.

A Most Respectable Gentleman
Whiteley's, Queensway, W2

Victorian father-figure slaughtered by son

William Whiteley, born of Yorkshire farming stock in 1831, personified the Victorian success story. He started in 1863 with a small clothes shop in Westbourne Grove, Bayswater, which he gradually expanded until it became the world's first 'department store'. He became known as the 'universal provider', and his store, *Whiteley's*, is still very much in business at the corner of Westbourne Grove and Queensway.

In the late 1880's his reputation became tarnished as a result of his unscrupulous business methods. He ruthlessly undercut local competitors and underpaid his staff who were ruled with an iron hand and forced to work an 84 hour week. His reputation also began to suffer from persistent rumours concerning the number of female employees he would seduce at his flat in Brighton. The final blow came in January, 1907, when a rather distraught young man came to see him in his office. After an interview lasting about 20 minutes the old man Whiteley came out of his room, his face

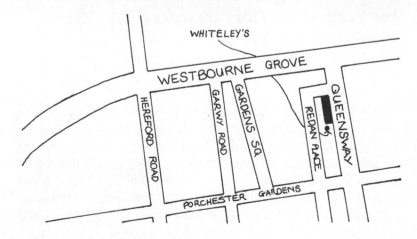

pale and anxious, and asked his secretary to call the police. The young man shouted to Whiteley to come back, and when he refused shot him through the head with his pistol. He then attempted to shoot himself but recovered from his wounds to stand trial for murder.

The young man, whose name was Horace Rayner, claimed he was Whiteley's illegitimate son, a fact not denied by the prosecution. His mother Emily and her sister Louisa had often visited Whiteley in Brighton at weekends, and when Louisa gave birth to a son, he made provision for her to receive £150 a year. No provision, however, had been made for Emily's son Horace. He explained that he had visited his father to beg for financial assistance and had threatened to commit suicide if refused. Whiteley had been so hard and unyielding that he was provoked into shooting him before turning the gun on himself. Horace was convicted of murder and sentenced to death, but as a result of public sympathy the sentence was commuted to 20 years imprisonment.

The Vampire of South Kensington
Gloucester Road, SW7

The acid-bath murders

In the basement of 79 Gloucester Road John Haigh would conduct his 'experiments': into a bath of sulphuric acid he would drop live mice and watch them as they slowly disintegrated. Here between 1944 and 1949 Haigh murdered at least four people and drank their blood before disposing of their bodies in the acid bath. His trial at Lewes Assizes in July 1949 attracted enormous publicity and his wax-work

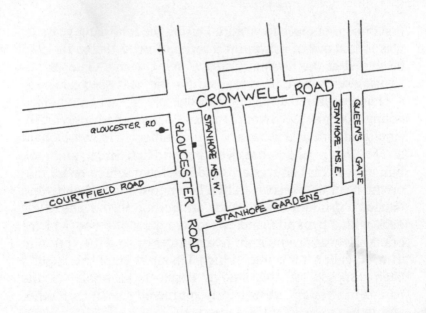

effigy is still looked for avidly in the Chamber of Horrors at
Madame Tussaud's.

Haigh was born in 1909. His parents were both members
of the Plymouth Brethren religious sect to whom all human
pleasure was sinful and even the reading of newspapers
frowned upon. John was brought up under the strictest
discipline and often subjected to paternal punishment. He
developed a strong sense of 'self-control' and recalled in later
life, 'the stubborn silence with which I greeted punishment
either by my parents or my tutors. I was always bitterly
resentful but I learnt not to show my feelings. I remained
superficially quiet but inside I was a boiling cauldron'.

As a young man he would have frequently recurring
dreams. In one he would see the body of Christ with blood
dripping from his wounds. In another, a forest of crucifixes,
would gradually change into trees and men would be
collecting something dripping from them. At first it was rain
or dew which, as the dream developed, turned into blood.
He tried to get near the men but could never get near enough
and felt an overwhelming desire for blood.

He married in 1934 but soon left his wife after serving his

21

first prison sentence for fraud. During the following years he was in and out of prison on a series of petty thefts. In 1943 he settled at the *Onslow Court Hotel*, Queen's Gate, South Kensington, where he remained for the next six years.

Haigh committed his first murder in 1944 when he killed young Donald McSwann, whose father had previously employed him as a secretary and chauffeur. He met Donald at *The Goat* public house, Kensington High Street, and took him back to his Gloucester Road basement where he hit him on the head with a cosh. 'Then I went out', said Haigh, 'and fetched a drinking glass, made an incision in the side of his neck with a penknife, and collected a glass of blood which I drank. He was dead within five minutes or so. I then put him in a 40-gallon tank into which I poured sulphuric acid. I later disposed of the sludge down a manhole in the basement'. Haigh subsequently murdered Donald's mother and father in exactly the same way.

A few months after killing Donald McSwann Haigh met a young woman about 35 years of age on Hammersmith Bridge and invited her back to his 'flat' in Gloucester Road. 'She came with me to the basement where I duly knocked her on the head with a cosh and tapped her for blood'. She too was disposed of in the acid bath.

Haigh also had a 'workroom' in Leopold Road, Crawley, which he had been allowed to use by a firm called Hurstlea Products. Here, too, he had an acid bath in which he dissolved several more victims.

In February 1949, Haigh invited a fellow guest at the Onslow Court Hotel, a Mrs Durand-Deacon, to visit his Crawley workroom. He shot her through the head, drank her blood and put her body in the acid tank. Accompanied by another hotel guest he went to the police on the following day to report Mrs Durand-Deacon missing. The police became suspicious of Haigh, however, and their investigations led to his Crawley workroom where they found traces of a human body that the acid had failed to obliterate: 28 lbs of body fat, part of a heel bone, a pelvis, an ankle, gallstones, and false teeth (some of which can still be seen in Scotland Yard's Black Museum). They also found Mrs Durand-Deacon's handbag.

On his arrest Haigh admitted to the murder but pleaded insanity. He was convicted, however, and hanged at Wandsworth Prison on the 6th August 1949. On the day of his execution he was greatly concerned over the appearance of his effigy at *Madame Tussaud's*. He directed that his own suit should clothe the figure, and sent it to the wax-works together with his green socks and red tie. He specially requested that the trousers be kept immaculately pressed!

79 Gloucester Road stands opposite the Gloucester Road Underground station and the basement can easily be seen from the street with a yard containing the drain down which Haigh's dissolved victims were poured. The basement rooms are now used for teaching English to foreign students.

The Sadist of Notting Hill
Pembridge Gardens, Notting Hill, W2

Another Jack the Ripper

A masochistic woman, it is said, can always recognise a sadistic man at a glance, and their mutual compatibility is sometimes the basis of a long and satisfying friendship. In the case of Margery Gardner and Neville Heath, however, things went too far.

Neville Heath, whose effigy can be seen at *Madame Tussaud's*, led the free-and-easy life of a con-man, passing dud cheques under various different names. During the Second World War he posed as Lieutenant Colonel N. G. C. Heath of the South African Air Force. He may have had a weak and sadistic character but he seems to have been

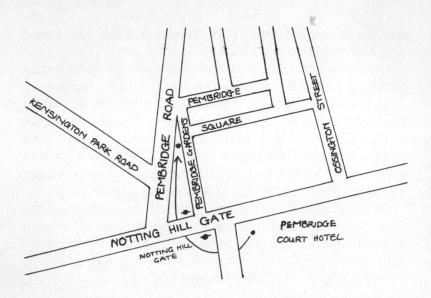

remarkably successful with women. In June 1946 he met Margery Gardner at *The Trevor Arms*, Knightsbridge. A 32 year old actress from a well-to-do family, living apart from her husband, she was enjoying a promiscuous life in Chelsea and took to the dashing Lieutenant Colonel immediately. They went back to his hotel room at the *Pembridge Court Hotel*, Pembridge Gardens, where she took off her clothes and lay on the bed. He then bound and gagged her and beat her so severely that she started to bleed. In the course of these perverted activities the unfortunate Margery was suffocated. Heath then assaulted her savagely. When her body was found her breasts had been almost bitten off, there were seventeen lash-marks on her face and body and her vagina had been torn by a rough instrument being thrust in and rotated.

The following Sunday a Group Captain Rupert Robert Brooke signed in at a hotel in Bournemouth and before midnight, with a speed reminiscent of the style of Lieutenant Colonel Heath, he had succeeded in picking up a young girl, Doreen Marshall, who was staying at a hotel nearby. The couple were seen to leave the hotel late at night and made their way to a local beauty spot, Branksome Dene Chine, where the girl's corpse was found on the following day. The body was naked except for one shoe, and had suffered the most appalling mutilation. She, too, had been bound and gagged, and Heath had stripped himself naked for his assault upon her. He killed her by cutting her throat, and then slashed her breasts and genitals with a knife. Like the victims of Jack the Ripper her body had been ripped open from the groin to the breastbone.

When the police interviewed 'Rupert Brooke' they recognised him as the missing Neville Heath and took him back to London to stand trial. He was found guilty of murder and hanged at Pentonville in October 1946.

The riding switch which Heath used on the body of Margery Gardner in that hotel room in Pembridge Gardens is exhibited in the *Black Museum* at the Metropolitan Police Headquarters, Victoria Street. The museum also contains the death masks of prisoners hanged at Newgate, the pyjamas in which Crippen wrapped parts of his wife's body, the wireless telegram that led to Crippen's arrest, and the heel-bone, gallstones and false teeth of Mrs Durand-Deacon that were spared by Haigh's sulphuric acid, and the gloves and gas-mask that Haigh used for his own protection. It also has the death mask of a murderer whose beard was shaved off prior to his execution in order to facilitate the hanging. Apparently the hairs about this death mask are still growing, and however much the Curator cuts them short they slowly continue to grow. Fortunately for the protection of public sanity, this museum is now only open to serving police officers.

Crippen
Hilldrop Crescent, Kentish Town, N7

American doctor poisons wife

Crippen was born in Michigan in 1861 and married a Polish Music Hall actress known as Belle Elmore. They came to England where he worked as a dentist and an agent for 'Munyon's Remedies', a patent-medicine firm. His wife appeared occasionally on the London stage and acted as Treasurer of the Music Hall Ladies' Guild.

The Crippens lived at 39 Hilldrop Crescent, Kentish Town, where, in January 1910, they gave a party. A few hours later Crippen poisoned his wife, cut up her body, burnt the bones and buried the remains in the cellar. He informed the Music Hall Ladies' Guild that his wife had returned to the United States. Suspicion was aroused, however, when six weeks later his young secretary, Ethel Le Neve, moved in with him. The couple appeared at the Ladies' Benevolent Fund Ball and it was noticed that Ethel was wearing Mrs Crippen's jewellery. In March Crippen announced his wife had died in California from pneumonia. Friends of the late Mrs Crippen became suspicious and alerted the police. In panic, Crippen and his girlfriend left for the continent. Mrs Crippen's remains were then discovered in the cellar.

At Antwerp the couple boarded a transatlantic liner bound for Quebec in the name of Robinson, father and son (Ethel Le Neve being dressed as a boy). They must have felt themselves safe at last but Crippen had not reckoned with the new invention of wireless. The ship's captain had read about the case and became suspicious of the feminine behaviour of Mr Robinson's 'son'. He sent a wireless message to Scotland Yard as a result of which Inspector Dew took a fast boat to Quebec and arrested the unsuspecting couple on landing. At their trial, Ethel Le Neve was acquitted and Crippen found guilty. He was hanged at

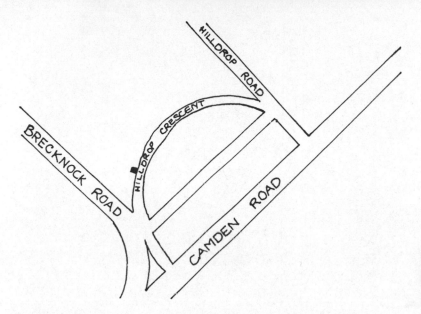

Pentonville on the morning of 23rd November 1910.

No. 39 Hilldrop Crescent has since been rebuilt as a block of flats, and the waste area built over, but Crippen's ghost is said to return each year to the grounds of the old house on the night of 31st January—the anniversary of the day his wife was killed.

Mary Pearcey
Ivor Street, Camden Town, NW1

Midwife murders lover's wife and baby

The sad figure of Mary Pearcey can be seen in the Chamber of Horrors at *Madame Tussaud's* with the contents of the flat she occupied in a depressing little terraced house at 2 Ivor Street, Camden Town. She earned her living as a midwife. Here, on the 24th October, 1890, she murdered the wife and infant daughter of her lover, Frank Hogg, who

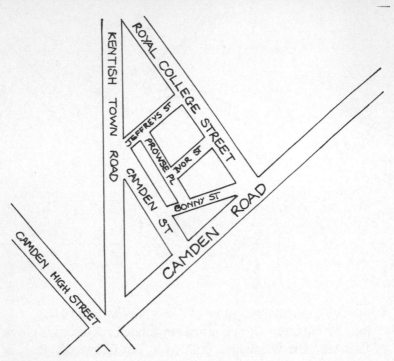

lived nearby in the Prince of Wales Road. Mary had known his wife, Phoebe, before they were married. She was also an old friend of his sister, and they had apparently remained on close terms even after the daughter was born, in spite of her affair with Frank.

On the 23rd October, 1890, Mary left a note at Phoebe's house asking her to call round with the baby. Phoebe visited Ivor Street with her daughter on the following day and was never seen alive again. Her body was found in Crossfield Road, Hampstead, dreadfully mutilated, with her neck cut through to the bone. The baby was found dead in St John's Wood. She had been suffocated. Here, too, the blood-stained pram was found. Fresh traces of blood in the kitchen at 2 Ivor Street revealed where the murder had been committed, and there were signs of a violent struggle. Mary was found guilty of murder and executed at Newgate on December 23rd.

A piece of toffee the baby had been chewing when suffocated is among the gruesome exhibits at *Madame Tussaud's*.

Seddon
Tollington Park, Holloway, N4

Insurance-broker poisons wealthy widow

Seddon and his wife were a most respectable couple. For 20 years he had been employed as an insurance agent by the London and Manchester Insurance Company. They lived at 63 Tollington Park, Holloway, and had converted the top floor of the house into a flat which they let to a rich and miserly old spinster, Miss Eliza Barrow. Seddon managed to persuade Miss Barrow to part with her money in exchange for an annuity and the use of the flat for the rest of her life. Shortly afterwards, Miss Barrow became ill and appointed Seddon sole executor under her will. Within a short time she died and was buried hurriedly in a common grave at Finchley Cemetery. Miss Barrow's relatives, none of whom were informed of her death, became suspicious and insisted that the body be exhumed. On examination, the corpse was found to contain traces of arsenic.

When charged with Miss Barrow's murder, Seddon replied, 'Scandalous! It's the first of our family that has ever been charged with such a crime'. He was found guilty and executed at Pentonville in April 1912. Ever since, the house

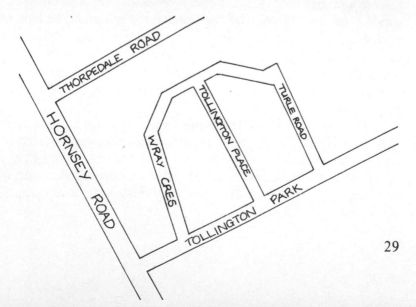

at 63 Tollington Park has been haunted by the sound of hurried footsteps on the stairs as if someone were going up and down in a state of great agitation. The house is now let out in furnished rooms to a constantly changing variety of tenants. They, too, have heard the footsteps but attribute them to the mice. By an understandable oversight the landlord forgot to tell them the full history of this unhappy house.

Brides in the Bath
Waterlow Road, Highgate, N19

Lady-killer marries three times

George Smith delighted in deceiving women and swindling them out of their money. He did this on several occasions before taking his technique a stage further and killing them.

In August 1910 he met Bessie Munday and induced her to marry him. They lived together for a short while before he ran off with her money. They met two years later at Weston-super-Mare and in spite of his desertion she agreed to live with him again. On July 8th, 1911, they made out wills in each other's favour and on the following day he took her to the doctor saying she'd had a fit. On July 13th Miss Munday was found drowned in the bath. Smith came into about £2,000 under her will.

In October, 1913, George Smith married Alice Burnham and insured her life for £500. They took their honeymoon in Blackpool where he complained to a local doctor about his bride's headaches. A few days later she was drowned in her bath and at the coroner's inquest a verdict of accidental death was recorded.

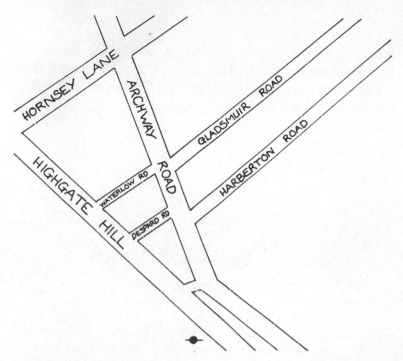

A year later, under the name of John Lloyd, he married Margaret Lofty, and this time took his bride to London for their honeymoon, staying in a room at 14 Waterlow Road, Highgate. True to form, they visited the doctor on account of Margaret's ill-health, and on the following day the bride was found dead in the bath. The *News of the World* picked up the sad story of the newly married couple's tragic accident and a policeman reading the paper noticed a certain similarity to the recent honeymoon tragedy in Blackpool.

George Smith was arrested and at his trial at the Old Bailey was defended by Marshall Hall, the most famous defence lawyer of his day. He was indicted for the murder of Bessie Munday at Herne Bay and the prosecution sought to produce evidence of the similar deaths of Alice Burnham and Margaret Lofty. Marshall Hall objected that such evidence was prejudicial to his client and irrelevant to the issue of *Bessie's* death but the presiding judge ruled that the evidence was admissible if it showed the accused had formed a habit of drowning young ladies in the bath in similar circumstances. This decision still constitutes an important authority in the English criminal law. George Smith was convicted and hanged. Both he and the old enamel bath taken from the house in Waterlow Road can be seen in *Madame Tussaud's* Chamber of Horrors.

The Nude Murders
Acton, Shepherd's Bush and Notting Hill

Girl's body found naked in Thames

The 'Nude Murders' hit the headlines in 1964. Another Jack the Ripper was at work killing one prostitute after another, but this time in the West End of London, around the Shepherd's Bush and Notting Hill areas.

The first victim was Hanna Tailford who was found naked in the Thames by Hammersmith Bridge with her stockings and panties forced into her mouth. She had been strangled. Two months later the naked body of another young prostitute, also strangled, was found near the boathouse in Duke's Meadow where Barnes bridge crosses the river. Yet another nude body was found shortly afterwards at Osterley Park: Helen Barthelemy, a 22 year old prostitute and part-time strip-tease artist. A post-mortem revealed that she had been choked in a most revolting and 'unnatural' manner. Her front teeth had been knocked in and traces of male sperm were found in her gullet. It was said she had been suffocated by the intrusion of the murderer's penis into her throat in the course of a repeated assault carried on both before and after her death.

A fourth body was found in Acton on the 14th July in the same condition as the others: naked, teeth missing and sperm in her throat. Finger marks and bruises indicated she

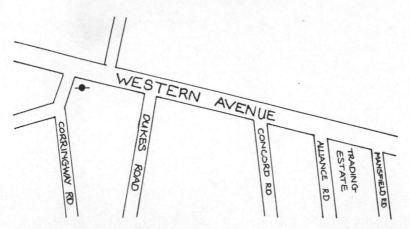

died in a kneeling position with her head held over the lap of the unknown murderer.

The fifth victim was Margaret McGowan, a Scots girl of 21 whose naked body was found in a carpark at Hornton Street near Campden Hill, Kensington. She had suffered the same awful fate as the others.

In February 1965 the body of Bridie O'Hara, a 28 year old prostitute who had last been seen about a month before at a Shepherd's Bush hotel, was found in some undergrowth on the trading estate at Alliance Road, off the Western Avenue, Acton. Again, teeth were missing, finger marks were found on the back of her neck and there were traces of sperm in her throat.

Particles of the same lead paint had been found on all the bodies. This led the police, after a long search, to a paint spray shop on the Alliance Road trading estate. It was here that the girls' dead bodies would be brought for the satisfaction of the murderer's perverted desires. The police suspected a security guard working on the estate who drove a van, worked nights, and had access to the paint shop. He committed suicide, however, before any charges were brought and the investigation was dropped. Several newspaper reporters covering the case were not convinced that the real murderer had been identified, particularly in view of the many rumours involving a prominent show-biz personality.

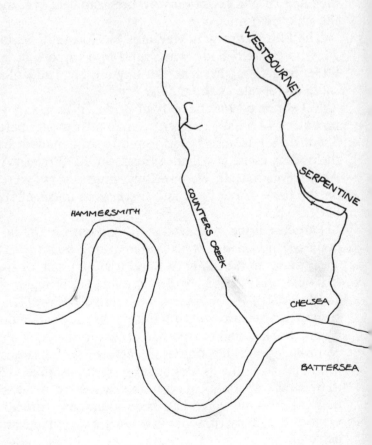

WESTBOURNE

SERPENTINE

HAMMERSMITH

COUNTERS CREEK

CHELSEA

BATTERSEA

Underground London

If the earth were transparent one would be able to see a maze of tunnels and pipes under London as well as sewers, railways, thousands of skeletons, underground rivers, the remains of ancient civilisations and a wealth of buried treasure.

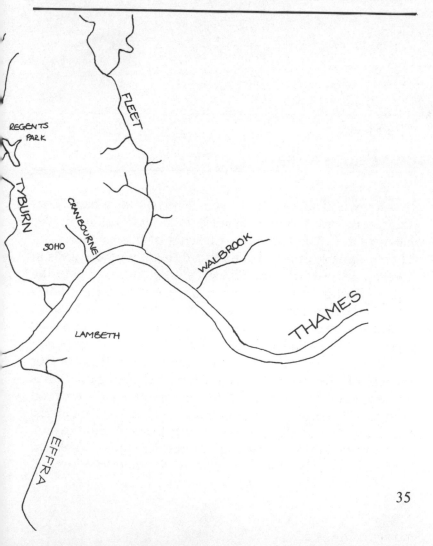

Lost Rivers of London

London's old rivers continue to flow underground

London's underground rivers make their presence felt in many unexpected ways: after heavy rainfall they cause local flooding; they burst through into building sites excavated in their paths; a permanent dampness affects the houses built over them; and they seem in some way to attract supernatural manifestations.

The Fleet

From Hampstead Heath to Fleet Street via King's Cross

Best known of all the 'lost rivers' is the Fleet, which flows vigorously towards the Thames in a vast tunnel under Farringdon Road. The highest reaches of this river can still be seen above ground on Hampstead Heath where it starts in a valley just east of *Jack Straw's Castle*, and runs into the Vale of Health. Joined by a tributary from the north it flows into the Hampstead Ponds and then goes underground at Southend Green. From here it runs under the north side of Fleet Road and Malden Road until it is joined, at the junction of Hawley Road and Kentish Town Road, by another branch of the river coming from the Highgate Ponds through Kentish Town. This other branch starts at Kenwood House, in the last surviving remnants of an ancient forest that once covered the whole of north London and beyond. At Camden Town it flows under the Regent's Canal and continues its way along the path of St Pancras Way and

Pancras Road, under King's Cross and along the valley, still clearly visible, occupied by Farringdon Road. It reaches the Thames just to the west of Blackfriars Bridge.

The banks of the Fleet valley below King's Cross were originally very steep, as one can still see from the gradient at which Great Percy Street runs down from Percy Circus to the King's Cross Road. Here the river appeared to flow through a hollow, and hence its old name at this part: Holbourne.

There were three bridges over the river: Holborn Bridge where the viaduct now stands, Middle Bridge where Fleet Lane joins Farringdon Street and the Fleet Bridge linking the east end of Fleet Street to Ludgate Hill. Below Fleet Bridge the river measured about 600 feet across, and was used as a dock. The name 'Seacoal Lane' running down by the old riverside near Ludgate Circus indicates that ships carrying coal would discharge their cargoes while moored in the Fleet. Even as high as Camden Town the river was 65 feet wide where it crossed under Kentish Town Road.

During the 17th and 18th centuries the river became known as Fleet Ditch, a filthy sewer into which much of London's refuse was discharged. So choked with sewage did it become that the water was turned into a thick sludge. In 1763 a man unfortunate enough to fall into the ditch was suffocated by the foul mud, and a barber from Bromley was found one cold winter morning stuck in the mud head first with his feet in the air and frozen to death. Pigs, however, would do rather well when lost in the Fleet, and a report of 1844 records how a Springfield butcher who lost a young boar in the Fleet Ditch was pleased to recover it some five months later well fattened and 'improved in price from 10/- to 2 gns'. There was apparently a whole tribe of wild pigs living underground in the Fleet towards Hampstead.

The Walbrook

Flows under the Bank of England

Flowing right through the heart of the old city, the Walbrook was the first of London's rivers to be buried underground. Its source was a large swamp, Moorfields, lying north of the City Wall, and the river began where Old Street now joins Shoreditch High Street. A tributary stream running under Middlesex Street joins the river at Broad Street station and another tributary from the west joins it at Blomfield Street. The valley of the river can be seen quite clearly at the Bank of England with Cheapside running down the west bank and Cornhill coming down the other side. During building work at the Bank in 1732 and in 1803 the river was discovered still trickling through the foundations of the building. It then flowed down to the Thames just west of the street called Walbrook reaching the river about 40 yards to the west of Cannon Street. The dip in Cannon Street marking the old river valley is very noticeable, though less steep than it was originally.

The Walbrook may have been navigable at its lowest reaches before the Roman City dammed up the river creating the swampy area of Moorfields and reducing the river to a relatively small stream only 14 feet wide. It would occasionally flood after heavy rainfall and in 1574 the river ran so swiftly that an 18 year old boy, attempting to jump it, fell in and was carried towards the Thames with such violence that no one could save him. Eventually 'he came against a cartwheel that stood in Dowgate (the inlet from the Thames) before which time he was drowned and stark dead'.

The Tyburn

Flows past Selfridges and Buckingham Palace

In Fitzjohn's Avenue, Hampstead, at the corner of Lyndhurst Road, is a fountain marking the site of the old Shepherd's Well — the source of the Tyburn River which flowed down through St John's Wood, Marylebone and Mayfair to the Thames at Westminster. The river is now completely covered over except at Regent's Park where it can be seen running into the boating lake. Unlike the Fleet which flows *under* the Regent's canal, the Tyburn is carried *over* the canal in a large iron conduit pipe which can be seen near the north west corner of the park west of St John's Wood roundabout.

In Oxford Street near *Selfridges* the valley of the Tyburn is clearly marked at Bond Street Tube station and the junction of Gilbert Street. Just north of Oxford Street the path of the river can be seen in the winding contours of Marylebone Lane which used to run along the east bank of the river. Between Oxford Street and Piccadilly the river crossed Brook Street at its lowest point, ran to the east of Berkeley Square near Bruton Lane, crossed Piccadilly where the river valley is clearly visible, and continued down the dip in Green Park, to Buckingham Palace at the bottom of Constitution Hill. Here water from the river was used to create the lake in St James's Park, and the old river can still be seen running along its narrow bed whenever the lake is drained for cleaning. Below Buckingham Palace the river flowed into marshland surrounding the old Thorny Island on which Westminster Abbey was built, and then into the Thames.

The Tyburn gave its name to Oxford Street which before the 18th century was known as Tyburn Road. It also gave its name, of course, to that notorious landmark 'Tyburn Tree', the three-sided gallows that stood for centuries at the junction of Oxford Street and Edgware Road.

The Westbourne

Forms the Serpentine in Hyde Park

In a delightful little corner of Hampstead Heath near the White Stone Pond, where children enjoy short donkey rides on summer weekends, is a curious steep-sided valley containing an area of swampy ground at the bottom and a slight trickle of water running under Branch Hill. This is the source of the Westbourne. Its original course can be seen in the old country road formed by Heath Drive, Cannon Hill and West End Lane. Here the river used to be called the Kilbourn, and crossed Kilburn High Road (the old Roman Watling Street) at Kilburn Park Road. It turns sharp left at Shirland Road which follows the course of the river to Formosa Street. Here it runs under Lord Hill's Road, crosses under Bishop's Bridge Road and runs to the west of Gloucester Terrace, across the Bayswater Road and into the Serpentine, a lake which was artificially created by damming up the Westbourne. From the Serpentine it again goes underground crossing Knightsbridge at Kinnerton Street, flowing under Cadogan Lane and Sloane Square, and joining the Thames at Chelsea Hospital, where its outfall can still be seen at low tide.

At the Sloane Square Underground station is an enormous rectangular iron pipe crossing the open air platforms a few yards above the heads of passengers. Thousands of people see it every day without giving a thought as to what it might be. Inside is the Westbourne on its way to the Thames.

Counter's Creek

Flows into the Thames at Chelsea Creek

A quarter of a mile up-river from Battersea Bridge, Chelsea Creek can be seen flowing into the Thames. This is the mouth of Counter's Creek, a stream which flows underground from Kensal Green Cemetery, Harrow Road. The river runs beneath Latimer Road, crossing under Holland Park Avenue at Shepherd's Bush roundabout. From here it flows south near Olympia along the course of the railway line, under Earl's Court exhibition, and under Stamford Bridge (the grounds of Chelsea Football Club).

The Mysterious Cranbourn

Puzzling river under Soho

The most mysterious of all London's underground rivers is the so-called 'Cranbourn' which flows towards the Thames under Cranbourn Street, Leicester Square. The stream used to feed 'Queen Elizabeth's Bath' at Charing Cross before it was closed in 1831. It also supplied water to a large tank under the stage of the Hippodrome Theatre now *The Talk of the Town*, at the corner of Cranbourne Street and Charing Cross Road, in the days when 'water shows' were put on there at the end of the last century. This strange river can also be seen through a grate in the basement of the *Mandrake Club* in Meard Street, Soho, running in a southerly direction.

What puzzles the experts on London's underground rivers and drainage is that the 'Cranbourn' or 'Cran' does not appear on any of the old maps of this area, nor is it to be found in the GLC's detailed sewer map. There is no record of it having ever existed as a natural stream before Soho was built over, and there is no trace of its ever being contained in a drain or sewer. Yet clearly it has been flowing through Soho to the Thames at Charing Cross for over 100 years!

The most convincing explanation is that it was originally an unlawful sewer, constructed in contravention of local bye-laws by Frith, the property speculator, who built much of Soho in the late 17th century and after whom Frith Street was named. It would have taken the sewage from Soho into an ancient drain known as 'Cock & Pye Ditch' that drained the marshland around Seven Dials into the Thames. This illicit sewer, and the steps taken to close it, are mentioned in the records of the Westminster Commissioners for Sewers. When proper sewers were dug the Cranbourn was abandoned to become just another lost watercourse under London.

Lost Rivers of South London

The Effra can still be seen at Dulwich

The land south of the Thames was always very flat and marshy, and the courses of its many rivers are therefore less noticeable. One of the larger rivers, however, the Effra, was comparable in size to the Fleet or the Westbourne. It started in the hilly regions of Dulwich and Norwood and flowed north through Brixton at the junction of Effra Parade and Dulwich Road. It then used to flow along the east side of Brixton Road to the Oval and into the Thames just west of Vauxhall Bridge Road. This river can still be seen above ground as an ornamental stretch of water in the garden of 'Belair' in Gallery Road, Dulwich.

The Lost Rivers Today

Underground rivers attract the Supernatural

In addition to inconvenience caused by the 'over-flow' of underground rivers after a heavy storm, when neighbouring streets and basements are often flooded, and the extra work involved on building sites when water-logged foundations need draining, the lost rivers have permanent effects on the population living above them. In particular, the incidence of rheumatism and chronic bronchitis is noticeably aggravated in the neighbourhood of the underground watercourses. A study of cases of bronchitis treated at Hampstead General Hospital showed that a large proportion of sufferers lived over or near the underground Fleet river where it flows through Kentish Town. It also appears that various allergies are associated with the course of underground rivers.

More surprising is the connection that has been shown to exist between underground rivers and supernatural phenomena. Of a hundred cases of ghosts and other hauntings reported since the mid-19th century, 75% occurred in houses over or near the old rivers, and this seems to be true of the hauntings mentioned in this guide. The connection between ghosts and underground water is not yet understood. Perhaps water under old houses causes sounds that are taken by the inhabitants to be supernatural, or the existence of underground water has some unexplained influence on the human mind.

The Post Office Railway

Little-known Underground through Central London

About 70 feet below ground level runs the Post Office railway, some 40 trains rumbling along 6¹/₂ miles of tunnel through the heart of Central London from Whitechapel in the east to Paddington in the west. It has eight railway stations: two are connected to Liverpool Street and Paddington main line stations, the others link up the Post Office sorting offices, including Mount Pleasant, Clerkenwell, one of the largest sorting offices in the world. At Paddington and Liverpool Street, where large consignments of mail arrive from the provinces and overseas, there are several openings giving access to shutes and conveyors which lead to the Post Office railway.

The platforms look much like those at ordinary Underground stations, though on a slightly smaller scale, the tracks being only 2ft gauge. The tunnels slope down from each station at a gradient of 1 in 20 and slope up again towards the next station, so that the carriages almost run on their own weight. Each carriage is 27ft long and could easily carry passengers, if this were ever permitted. At the moment, unfortunately, it is not; the line is closed to the public.

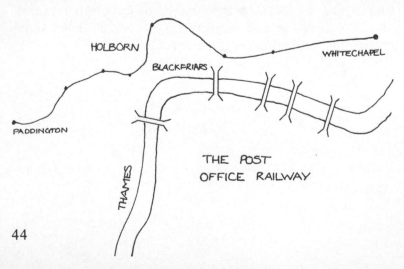

HOLBORN

BLACKFRIARS

WHITECHAPEL

PADDINGTON

THAMES

THE POST
OFFICE RAILWAY

Strange Burials

Corpses under London's crossroads

Under many crossroads in London lie the bones of people who committed suicide. Their sin did not permit a religious burial in consecrated ground, and instead, by ancient custom, their bodies would be thrown into a pit at the nearest crossroad and a stake driven through their hearts.

Perhaps the most famous suicide burial was that of John Williams, a seaman accused of the murder of the Marr and Williamson families in Wapping. Thomas de Quincey wrote about it in his essay *On Murder Considered as one of the Fine Arts*.

Late at night on the 7th December, 1811, Marr, his wife, their infant son and a 13 year old apprentice who lived with them at their house in The Highway were all found by a servant battered to death lying on the floor with their throats cut. Again on the 19th December the owner of *The King's Arms* pub, a Mr Williamson, together with his wife and their servant Bridget were found by the lodger killed in the same brutal fashion. From the top of the stairs the lodger had managed to catch a glimpse of the murderer, whose seasman's hammer was found by the bodies covered with blood. On Christmas Eve the chief suspect, John Williams, was arrested. He had been seen at the pub on the night of the murder and his blood-stained shirt had been sent to be cleaned the next day. Two days later, when the magistrates sent for him, he was found dead in his cell hanging from a bar by his neckerchief.

His burial on New Year's Eve was a dramatic event. Attended by 300 constables, their swords drawn, his body was placed on a cart raised for public view on a platform 6 feet high. The procession moved along The Highway, stopping at the Marrs' House and The King's Arms, until it reached the junction of Cannon Street Road and Cable Street, where a large pit had been prepared. Surrounded by

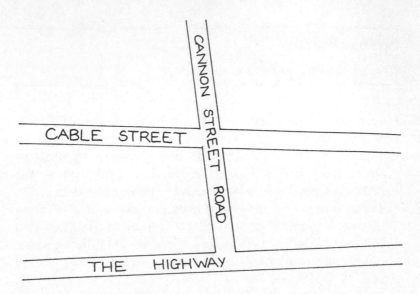

thousands of spectators, Williams' body was thrown into this hole and a stake driven through his heart with the same hammer that had been used in the murders. The grave was then filled with quick lime and covered over. About 100 years later when drains were being laid here the murderer's bones were discovered and removed by the criminologist, Churton Collins.

Similar scenes were frequently repeated at crossroads all over London until the ancient custom was ended by a special Act of Parliament rushed through at the request of George IV in 1823. The King's coach had been delayed by one of these macabre rituals at the junction of Hobart Place and Grosvenor Place on the south west corner of the Buckingham Palace gardens, while the body of a young man who had committed suicide after murdering his father was being buried. King George was not amused by the thought of a corpse lying so close to Buckingham Palace and it was also widely felt that with the growth of London's traffic such obstructions to the highway were no longer tolerable.

Buried Treasure

London's hidden wealth

The only safe thing to do with your valuables during the more turbulent periods of English history was to bury them underground and keep the secret of their location to yourself. Even as late as 1666, during the Fire of London, we note that Samuel Pepys buried his gold and silver in his father-in-law's garden at Bethnal Green. Many private citizens who adopted this method of safe-keeping, however, had the misfortune to die unexpectedly and the secret of the treasure's whereabouts died with them.

The burying of treasure was particularly prevalent at times of unrest or civil war. It was also undertaken on a large scale at the time of the Reformation when King Henry VIII was busy laying his hands on the wealth of the monasteries. To forestall this royal plunder the monks would hide a portion of their most valuable jewels and religious treasures in the hope that one day the Church's troubles would be over and its property restored. These hopes were not fulfilled, and in the following years their buried treasures were discovered. A tremendous hoard was found, for example, in a deep cellar under Long Acre in a large iron-bound chest. It contained jewels and gold and silver coins from the time of Henry VIII, and had probably been taken by the monks of Westminster Abbey from the Abbot's treasury and buried in the grounds of the convent that used to occupy what is now Covent Garden.

Tothill Street SW1

Stolen silver from the Royal Palace

When the old *Cock & Tabard* pub in Tothill Street, Westminster, was being demolished in 1871 a valuable collection of silver plate was found at the rear of the premises. Judging by its magnificence and great value it had been stolen from the Royal Palace. Tothill Street in the 18th Century was another of the squalid slums like St Giles, Clare Market and Wapping where the London underworld tended to congregate. Many thieves who buried their loot in such places would eventually hang at Tyburn leaving their ill-gotten gains unclaimed beneath the ground. This would explain the Tothill treasure and there must be many more like this in the areas of these old 18th century slums.

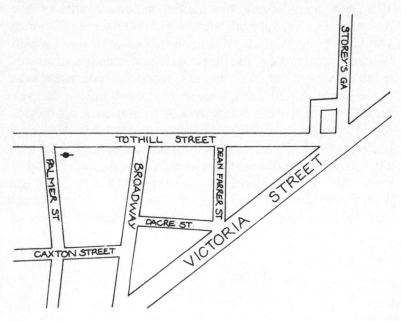

Hounslow Heath

Hidden loot of highwaymen

Similar hoards have been found near old Hounslow Heath, the scene of frequent highway robberies between 1650 and 1800. By the mid-18th century it was dotted with gallows and the decayed carcasses of highwaymen hanging in the wind. This was the haunt of the famous James Maclean (model for Gay's Captain MacHeath in the *Beggar's Opera*), Jack Shepherd, '16 String Jack', and other notorious Gentlemen of the Road. It was always rumoured that the money and other valuables taken by these men were hidden in taverns around the Heath, some of which still remain: *The Peggy Bedford*, Bath Road, Hillingdon; *The Green Man*, Green Man Lane, Hatton; *The Three Magpies*, Bath Road, Heathrow, and *The Bell* at 2 Staines Road, Hounslow.

At the Peggy Bedford a large quantity of valuable coins dating from the 17th and 18th centuries was found recently under the floorboards. A search at The Green Man revealed a cavity behind the fireplace containing old buckles and clay pipes. And at The Three Magpies, where a Captain Mellish died after being attacked by highwaymen in 1798, there is said to be buried treasure at the bottom of a deep well sunk into the floor of the Inn.

Clay Hill, Enfield

Dick Turpin's Treasure

Dick Turpin, the famous highwayman who rode from London to York in one day on his horse Black Bess, operated to the north of the city in an area stretching from Hampstead

Heath to Enfield Chase. His grandfather kept a pub called *The Rose and Crown* near Clay Hill, Enfield, where Turpin would often stay when he needed a retreat. Here Turpin hid his vast treasure accumulated during his short but successful career as a burglar, highwayman and cattle thief. No one has yet succeeded in finding it, however, although treasure-hunters have searched in the vicinity of the old Rose and Crown.

Trent Park, Enfield

Earl of Essex's treasure chest

Within Turpin's old haunts lies Trent Park, Barnet, the site of another unfound treasure. An ancient well in a corner of Camlet Moat is believed to have a false stone bottom containing an iron treasure chest that belonged to Geoffrey de Mandeville, first Earl of Essex, who lived in a Manor-House here in the 12th century. The Earl hid his treasure in the well when he had to go into hiding after being suspected of treason against the King. He died shortly afterwards in battle while besieging Burwell Castle, Cambridgeshire.

There is no record of the treasure ever having been found, though it would be surprising if no search has been made at some time during the 800 years that have elapsed since the Earl's death. A problem that would have faced any treasure-hunter, however, is the presence of a ghostly sentry—said to be the Earl himself—who apparently stands guard over the well protecting its secrets against unauthorised intruders.

Haunted London

London is the most haunted city in the world. It always has been. Some ghosts have been known in places like the Tower of London and Westminster Abbey since the Middle Ages; others have appeared in recent times. Those mentioned here have been seen or heard so often they have become part of London's supernatural history.

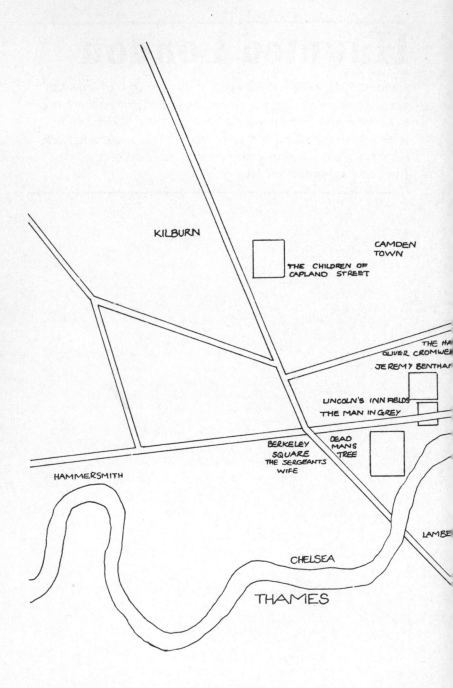

KILBURN

CAMDEN TOWN

THE CHILDREN OF CAPLAND STREET

THE HA
OLIVER CROMWEI
JEREMY BENTHAM

LINCOLN'S INN FIELDS
THE MAN IN GREY

DEAD MANS TREE

BERKELEY SQUARE
THE SERGEANTS WIFE

HAMMERSMITH

LAMBE

CHELSEA

THAMES

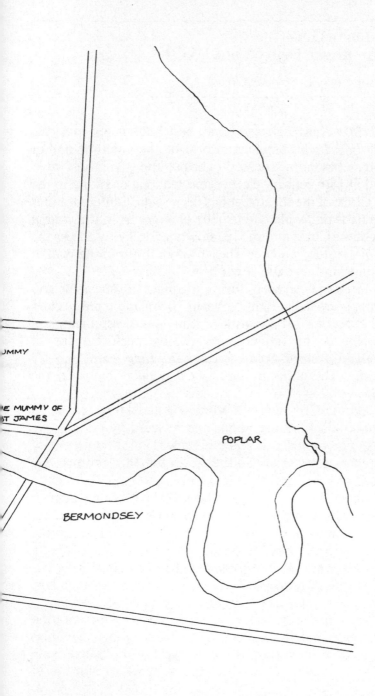

MMY

E MUMMY OF
ST JAMES

POPLAR

BERMONDSEY

The Man in Grey
Theatre Royal, Drury Lane, WC2

The haunting of the Upper Circle

The Theatre Royal, Drury Lane, best known for musicals like *My Fair Lady,* happens also to be the haunt of one of London's best-authenticated ghosts the 'Man-in-Grey'. Dressed in 18th century clothes and walking or sitting in the Upper Circle of the theatre, it has been seen at different times by hundreds of people. He usually emerges from the wall at the left of the Circle and moves slowly and silently across the rear of the seating, and vanishes through the opposite wall of the auditorium near the royal box.

He has often been seen during matinees or rehearsals and usually appears in daylight between 10 am and 6 pm. Actors say his appearance at a matinee means a successful run, and they point to his attendances during performances of *Oklahoma, Carousel, South Pacific, The King and I,* and *My Fair Lady.* The ghost is naturally a popular figure in the theatre.

The Man-in-Grey wears a white wig and a three-cornered hat, a short cloak, riding boots, and a sword by his side. He appears to be young, and it is said he was in love with one of the popular actresses at the theatre in the 18th century. He would sit in the Upper Circle during rehearsals in order to watch his beloved on stage. The seductive young actress, however, was also the theatre manager's mistress, and the rivalry between the two lovers ended in a duel in which the young man was stabbed to death. To avoid scandal his body was bricked up in a little passage off the Upper Circle. His miserable ghost returns to the scene of his tragic affair, endlessly yearning for a glimpse of the faithless actress.

The ghost has been seen so often in recent years that it no longer causes much surprise. In 1938 a cleaner saw him during a rehearsal sitting in the end seat of the fourth row. Thinking he was an actor she went to speak to him but as

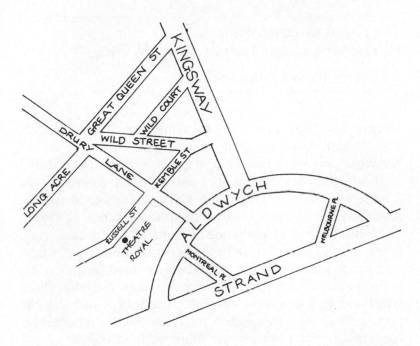

she approached he got up, moved away and vanished into the wall. During a matinee performance of *Carousel* in 1950 the leading actor, Morgan Davies, also saw the Man-in-Grey seated in one of the empty boxes. The unearthly spectator occupied the box for about 10 minutes before vanishing. Occasionally members of the audience will ask whether actors often come out and join them in the Upper Circle because they sometimes notice a theatrically dressed young man sitting nearby.

Around 1850, workmen at the theatre came across a part of the main wall which sounded hollow. They broke through and found a small room, seemingly part of a disused passage, containing a human skeleton. The bones were judged to be those of a young man, and inside the rib-cage Was a dagger! This secret chamber was located at the very place where the ghost always disappeared into the wall. The identity of the body was never discovered. Its remains were buried in an old graveyard which is now Drury Lane Gardens at the corner of Russell Street and Drury Lane.

The Ghost of Jeremy Bentham
University College, Gower Street, WC1

Embalmed Mummy haunts college

Jeremy Bentham was born in Houndsditch, London, in 1748, and became famous for his philosophy of 'utilitarianism'—the belief that what is good is what is useful in the furtherance of human pleasure. He was one of the founders in 1826 of University College, Gower Street, the first university to be established in London. When he died in 1832 his body was embalmed, as he had requested, and preserved in University College. You can still see him there, inside a glass case near the entrance hall. He sits at ease in his favourite chair, wearing his own clothes complete with white gloves and a walking stick. Bentham hoped that the presence of his mummified remains would ensure his continuing influence over the affairs of the College.

His continuing presence is indeed still felt—but as a ghost. He has been seen and heard many times walking the lonely corridors on dark winter evenings. Some years ago, a mathematics teacher, Neil King, working late into the night,

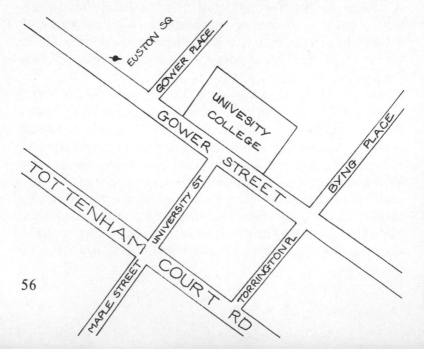

heard the distant echo of a walking stick tapping in the corridor. He opened the door and was amazed to see Jeremy Bentham coming towards him, dressed in the embalmed figure's clothes and wearing white gloves. When it was no further than about two yards, the ghost suddenly reached forward as if to seize him. Just when the terrified Mr King expected to be thrown to the ground, he found himself alone. The spectre of Jeremy Bentham had disappeared.

It seems that Jeremy Bentham's ghost must be searching for something—information perhaps, that could finally set his soul at rest. Books are often disturbed for no apparent reason, and volumes are found lying open in the morning which had been firmly on their shelves the previous day.

The Ghost of Lincoln's Inn Fields
Lincoln's Inn Fields, WC2

Black Magic for Mary Queen of Scots

Lincoln's Inn Fields, Holborn, was a frequent resort of Roman Catholics during the persecution of their religion in the 16th and 17th centuries. At *The Ship Tavern*, a pub that still stands in Little Turnstile at the north west corner of the square, religious services were held in secret. Worshippers would take a mug of ale at the bar and pass into the parlour, and a waiter would keep watch at the door. At any sign of danger the priest would disappear into a specially constructed hiding place upstairs while the congregation continued merely drinking and talking amongst themselves.

The ghost of a prominent Catholic continues to haunt Lincoln's Inn Fields to this day: that of Anthony Babington, who was executed there in 1586. In 1580 he had joined a secret society to protect Jesuit missionaries, and by 1586 was

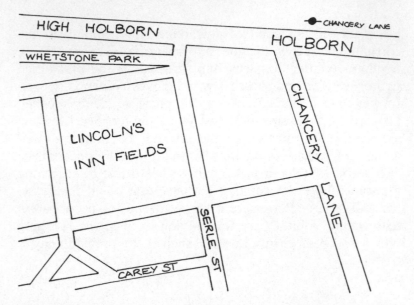

conspiring with other Catholics to murder Queen Elizabeth and rescue Mary Queen of Scots. Letters between Babington and Mary plotting Elizabeth's murder were discovered and Babington went into hiding. A wax figure of Queen Elizabeth pierced with pins—supposedly evidence of some black magic ritual—was discovered in Lincoln's Inn Fields, which was therefore regarded as the scene of the conspiracy. Anthony Babington was eventually captured at Harrow, tried with 13 of his accomplices and condemned to be hanged, drawn and quartered. Execution was carried out on the 20th September in Lincoln's Inn Fields, and Froude, describing the execution, wrote: 'they were hanged but for a moment, according to the letter of the sentence, taken down whilst the susceptibility of agony was unimpaired and cut in pieces afterwards with due precautions for the protraction of the pain'. When told of this barbarous cruelty, Queen Elizabeth forbade its repetition and the rest of the conspirators were hanged until they were dead before being quartered.

For many years afterwards anguished screams were heard coming from the centre of the square and the ghost of Anthony Babington was said to appear near the site of his execution. His ghost would also haunt *The Ship Tavern*, but there has been no sign of him there in recent years.

In the 18th century, Lincoln's Inn Fields was a rough and dangerous place, frequented by 'wicked and disorderly persons', where 'rebellious assaults, outrages and enormities have been and continually are, committed'. Today it is very respectable, with the Royal College of Surgeons occupying the south side, lawyers on the east and the *New Statesman* on the north east corner at Great Turnstile. It also provides healthy entertainment, with tennis courts and netball facilities in constant use by buxom, long-legged schoolgirls in their mini-gymslips. The square is always crowded with spectators, and an unusual interest in netball is shown by the local raincoated fraternity.

The Ghost of Oliver Cromwell
Red Lion Square, WC1

Cromwell's corpse disinterred

Before Red Lion Square was built in 1698 the area was known as Red Lion Fields, the site at one time of a gallows. The bodies of those hanged here, and of those hanged at Tyburn, were often buried without ceremony in these fields. Not even a simple wooden stake would be left to honour the dead.

The most famous body to be ditched in these grounds was that of Oliver Cromwell, who died in 1658. Severe reprisals followed the restoration of the monarchy in 1660 against those who had been active in the parliamentary cause and who had taken part in the trial and execution of Charles I. The bodies of Oliver Cromwell, Henry Ireton (Cromwell's son-in-law) and John Bradshaw (who had pronounced the

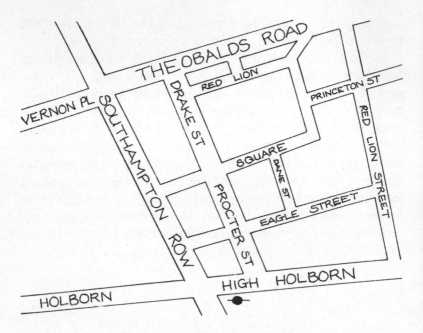

King's death sentence) were disinterred from where they lay in Westminster Abbey and hanged by their rotting necks at Tyburn for the offence of regicide. Having been duly punished, the corpses were cut down, mutilated, and thrown into unconsecrated ground at Red Lion Fields.

Such disrespect for the dead had its inevitable consequence: for many years the ghosts of the three men would be seen walking together in Red Lion Fields three abreast, deep in conversation. They were still seen occasionally after the Fields were built on, and the square laid out, in 1698. However, they would follow their old path, walking deliberately through walls and fences as if the new buildings had never been erected. During the First World War a constable attached to Holborn police station approached three men in Red Lion Square who appeared to be wearing fancy dress. He did not get within 20 yards of them, however, before they vanished, seeming to disappear into the wall at Lamb's Conduit Passage.

The Mystery of the Haunted Mummy
British Museum, Great Russell Street, WC1

The famous 'curse of the Mummy's tomb'

In the second Egyptian room, on the first floor of the British Museum, is exhibit number 22542, bearing the following label: 'Mummy cover from the coffin of an unknown princess from Thebes. 21st Dynasty'. The beautiful face of a woman decorates the outer surface.

This coffin lid is said to carry the famous 'curse of the Mummy's tomb'. Sir Wallis Budge, former Keeper of Egyptian and Assyrian Antiquities in the British Museum, believed, apparently, that the man who discovered the Mummy fell dead as soon as he touched the cloth in which it had been wrapped for over 3,000 years. Sir Wallis also

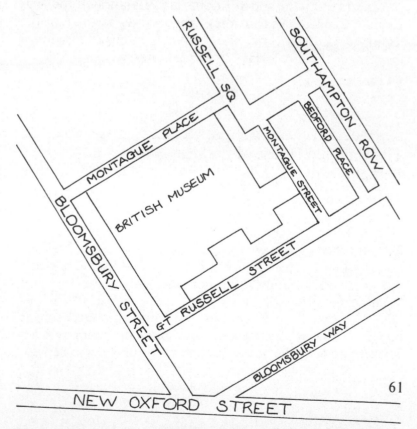

believed that a photographer who took several pictures of the coffin died suddenly soon afterwards, and that the photographs, when processed, revealed not the calm composed face that appears on the lid but the contorted face of a woman in torment with a look of terror in her eyes. Mysterious and unnerving noises could sometimes be heard coming from the exhibit; the sound of hammering, for example, and of a woman weeping.

Another story relates how the British Museum authorities, anxious to be rid of the troublesome coffin lid, sold it to a museum in New York; how it was shipped on board the *Titanic* on its maiden voyage; how it was salvaged by survivors and taken to America when the ship struck an iceberg and sank; how a succession of disasters followed it wherever it went; and how, eventually, it returned to England as the gift of wealthy Canadian to take its place once again in the British Museum.

Visitors to the Egyptian Rooms are often drawn towards Exhibit 22542, even if they have never heard of the 'Haunted Mummy', and many report a strange sensation if they linger there too long!

The Haunted House of Berkeley Square
Berkeley Square, W1

Death in a small top room

One hundred years ago No. 50 Berkeley Square was the most famous haunted house in London. The Square was laid out in 1698 and distinguished residents have included William Pitt, Earl of Chatham, (No. 6); Horace Walpole, (No. 11); and Lord Clive (No. 45)—he committed suicide here in 1774. No. 50 was occupied for many years by a Mr Myers who took the house just before his intended marriage.

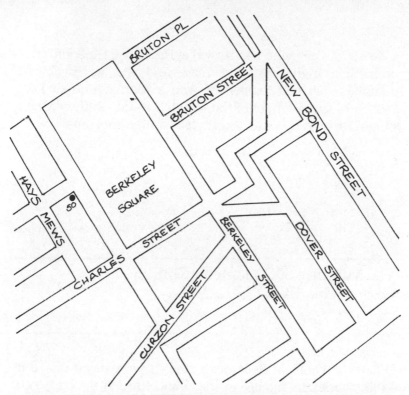

At the last minute his fiancee changed her mind, and poor Mr Myers was left to occupy the house alone for the rest of his life. He lived as a hermit in a small top room and his shadow was now and then seen against the closed curtains as he shuffled round the room late at night. He never allowed a woman to set foot in the house and only his manservant kept him company.

After Myers' death the house often stood empty and in the 1870's became notorious for its ghosts who were said to haunt the small top room. In 1872 Lord Lyttleton, as a bet, agreed to spend a night alone in this room. As a precaution he took with him two shotguns and some silver coins to ward off evil. Near dawn, after a sleepless night, he saw something moving towards him. In panic, he picked up a gun, aimed it at the threatening form and fired. In the morning he and his friends looked for what he had shot, but nothing could be found, dead or alive, apart from the bullets that had entered the wall.

In 1879 a girl who had stayed at the house experienced so dreadful a fright she went mad, and was never able to describe what had happened. And a man who, like Lord Lyttleton, spent a night in the haunted room—but without a shotgun or silver—was found dead in the morning.

The Mummy of St. James's Church Garlick Hill, EC4

Body found in City church

When the vaults of St James's church were being closed in 1839, workmen digging in the chancel found the body of a man, embalmed at least 400 years earlier, in a state of perfect preservation. His identity was not known, but he must have been important since it was rare in the Middle Ages to embalm the bodies of the dead. He may have been one of the six Lord Mayors of London who were buried in this church, including Henry FitzEylwin, the first mayor, who died in 1212. Some say it is Dick Whittington himself although he is supposed to have been buried in the church of St Michael Paternoster Royal.

Since his discovery, the mummy has not really been treated with the respect he obviously deserves. In the 1880's the choir boys, for a laugh, used to take him for a run around the church. Today he can be seen in a glass case off the porch and is referred to jokingly as 'Old Jimmy Garlick'.

The misused old mummy gets his own back by frightening unsuspecting visitors, appearing as a tall, brooding figure draped in a white sheet with arms folded, utterly motionless and silent. He was seen several times

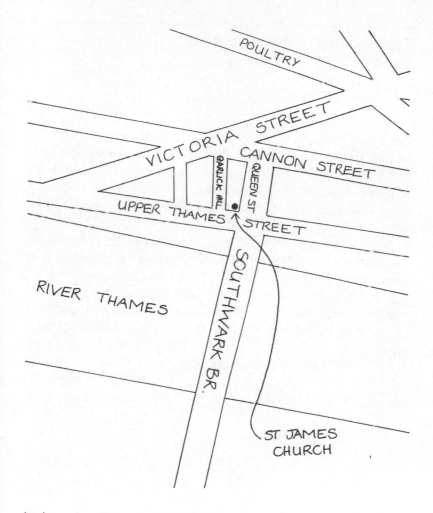

during the Second World War and on one occasion a fireman told him to take shelter during an air raid, whereupon he simply melted away. An American visitor who brought her two sons to see the church recently seems to have encountered the ghost when her eldest boy for no apparent reason became suddenly frightened and dragged her from the church. They knew nothing about the mummy and had not heard about the ghost but the boy described a corpse he had seen on the balcony of the church wearing a sheet over his head and appearing to pray.

The Children of Capland Street
Capland Street, NW8

Victims of poverty

For many years Capland Street, off Lisson Grove, St John's Wood, has been said to be haunted by the unhappy sound of children crying. Usually heard at night, the cries are faint and die away after a few minutes. Occasionally, however, a terrible scream will be heard above the crying, as if a child was in fear for his life.

Some local residents believed the area to be haunted by the ghosts of children who died in an old orphanage that used to stand between Lisson Grove and Edgware Road. Of this orphanage, however, there is no record. Among older residents it was said that the sounds were made by the ghosts of children murdered by their father about 100 years ago. Apparently, a cobbler named Nicholls lived in Capland Street, with his wife and six children. He worked at a nearby shoe factory in the Edgware Road. One Saturday night for no reason, and without prior warning, he was dismissed.

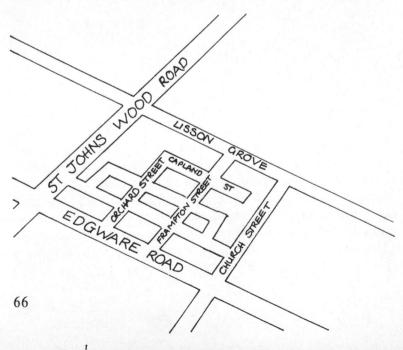

Being a poor man, already in debt, with a large family to support, he was shattered by this unexpected blow. On the following Monday, after his wife had gone out, he sent the two eldest children on an errand. Then, with his cobbler's knife, he cut the throats of the four youngest children before committing suicide himself. At the inquest it was recorded that he killed his children and himself while his mind was 'unhinged from the pressure of poverty'.

Dead Man's Tree
Green Park, SW1

Suicides in old Tyburn Valley

Dead Man's Tree stands about fifty yards from Piccadilly, almost in front of the *Park Lane Hotel*, about ten yards west of the junction between two footpaths. It is a large sinister-looking Plane tree, covered with ugly growths on its trunk, and has a strange hole in its side about twelve feet from the ground. Beneath it runs the old Tyburn river. Its reputation dates from the early 18th century when many fatal duels were held beneath its wide-spreading branches. During the 19th century it became known for suicides, usually committed by hanging from the lowest branch.

Within the last 100 years rumours began to grow that the tree was haunted. The pale figure of a tall bearded young man wearing a frock coat, would be seen in the late evening beside the tree for just a few brief minutes before vanishing. He was never seen to approach the tree or to leave it, and was said to be the ghost of a young man who shot himself through the heart at this spot in about 1820 after his wife and four children had been killed in a fire. It is also said that in the stillness of night, when the traffic along Piccadilly has

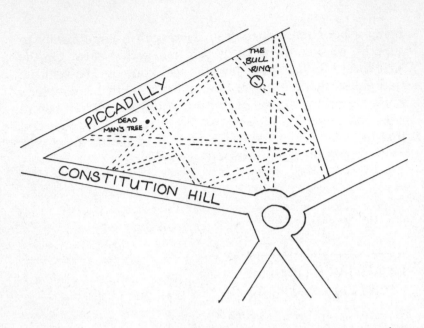

departed, a low and mournful sigh can be heard coming from the tree, like the sound of a man in despair. The atmosphere is certainly unwelcoming. Children play elsewhere, and animals, who are sensitive to such things, tend not to approach it.

Another unfortunate area of Green Park, where several bodies have been found in recent years, is the so-called 'bull ring'—a circular opening in the footpath leading from Piccadilly to the Mall where a small police box now stands. There are no reports, however, of any hauntings at this spot.

The Ghost of the Sergeant's Wife
Birdcage Walk, St. James's Park, SW1

Jealous sergeant decapitates wife

St James's Park was created by Henry VIII out of land seized from the Abbot of Westminster. During the reign of James I it was laid out as the park we know today, and the lake was re-designed in its present form by the architect, John Nash.

This lake is said to be haunted by the headless ghost of a woman that runs across the grass lawns near Birdcage Walk. She was the wife of a sergeant of the Coldstream guards, whose body was found in the lake in 1816. The couple lived at Wellington Barracks nearby, and the sergeant had stabbed her to death and severed her head from her body after suspecting her of having an affair with another guardsman. He had carried her body along Birdcage Walk during the night and thrown it into the lake. Her head was found buried in the Barrack grounds.

The headless apparition is usually seen running towards Cockpit Steps, wearing a long blood-stained dress and dripping with water. One witness nearly hit the ghost recently as he was driving along Birdcage Walk in the early hours of the morning.

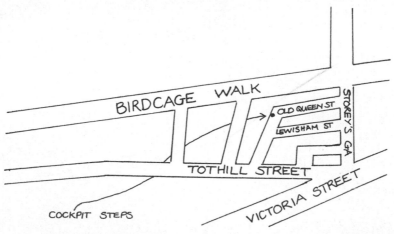

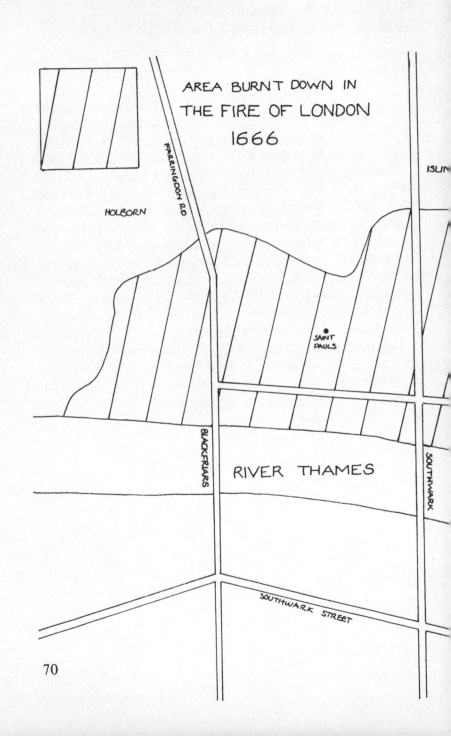

AREA BURNT DOWN IN
THE FIRE OF LONDON
1666

ISLIN

HOLBORN

FARRINGDON RD

SAINT
PAULS

BLACKFRIARS

SOUTHWARK

RIVER THAMES

SOUTHWARK STREET

Mysterious London

Ancient curses seem to plague the city. Weird stones and monuments exert strange and unknown powers. And riddles of history remain unsolved. London is full of mysteries. Some of the most puzzling are described in this section.

The Riddle of the Fire of London
The City

Was the fire really an accident?

In the City near London Bridge stands *The Monument* erected to commemorate the Great Fire of London, 1666. Only six people were killed but the old medieval town was reduced to ashes. Not even the mighty St Paul's Cathedral was spared.

The inscription on the north side of the monument provides a fascinating clue to an unsolved riddle of the fire. At the end of a brief history of the fire is a mysterious blank space where words have been obliterated by chipping away the stone. Having described how the flames died out, the inscription originally said: 'the Popish frenzy, which caused such horrors, is not yet quenched'. These words have been deleted.

Another inscription, also deleted, used to tell how 'the burning of this Protestant city was began and carried on by the treachery and malice of the Popish faction in order for carrying on their horrid plot for extirpating the Protestant and old English liberty and introducing Popery and slavery'.

The Fire was a severe blow to the people of London, destroying their property and possessions and rendering over 80,000 homeless. No-one believed that such a fire could have been an accident. It started at the home of the King's baker in Pudding Lane in the early hours of Sunday 2nd September, 1666, and burned for three days assisted by a strong east wind. London had seen many fires, but this one seemed to spread with unusual rapidity, often flaring up in houses some distance from the main fire. People were convinced that it was started and deliberately spread by either the French, the Dutch or the 'Papists'.

After the Fire an investigation was conducted by a committee of Parliament which found much evidence to support the conspiracy theory. Pepys thought the evidence of a plot was 'very plain'. A young Frenchman, Richard Hubert, admitted starting the fire deliberately on instructions from an organisation in France who paid him to do so. He was hastily convicted and hanged before a proper investigation could be conducted, in spite of Parliament's request to examine him. It looked as though the King was trying to suppress evidence. Proceedings of the Parliamentary committee of inquiry were officially published and put on sale to the public but were immediately ordered by the King to be burnt. Before the Parliamentary committee could make its final report, Parliament was dissolved by the King and the committee was never revived. Its chairman, Sir Robert Brook, had an 'accident' on a French ferry soon afterwards and was drowned.

The unusual ferocity of the Fire and its rapid progress through the City, together with the strange suppression of evidence afterwards, remained a mystery and a subject of contention between Catholics and Protestants for many years. However, with the decline in religious conflict during the 19th century, the issue was forgotten.

Whatever its cause—whether deliberate or accidental— the Fire of London had an effect on the City that we can see to this day. It enabled the architect, Christopher Wren, to rebuild the City churches, including the magnificent Cathedral of St Paul's. But its destruction of the old town also explains why there is virtually nothing left of medieval London, save the names and layout of its streets.

The Curse of Cleopatra
Victoria Embankment, WC2

Death in the Thames

The ancient Egyptian obelisk on the Victoria Embankment near Waterloo Bridge has always been associated with the suicide of Cleopatra in 30 B.C., a few days after the death of her lover, Mark Antony. Ever since, the obelisk, which dates back to the reign of Thothmes III, 1500 B.C., has carried 'Cleopatra's Curse'.

When British influence was established in Egypt after Nelson's victory in the Battle of the Nile, the Viceroy of Egypt was glad to offer the obelisk to George IV. Wisely, this offer was not accepted. It was offered again to successive British monarchs with the added inducement that it would be shipped to England free of charge. Each time the offers were declined. Eventually a Greek merchant who had acquired the land on which the obelisk stood, insisted upon its removal, and in 1877 it was put on board a tug bound for England. En route, a terrible storm blew up and Cleopatra's Needle had to be abandoned. Six sailors were drowned. In spite of this tragedy, however, the attempt to bring the ill-fated obelisk to England was resumed, and in 1878 it was triumphantly erected in its present position.

Unfortunately, the curse of Cleopatra's Needle has continued to exercise its uncanny fascination. According to the River Police there are more suicides and attempted suicides in the vicinity of the obelisk than on any other stretch of the Thames. The eerie sound of mocking laugher has also been heard echoing across the muddy river banks which are exposed (and accessible) here at low tide.

With a conceit and self-confidence for which one must admire the Victorians in their hey-day, the Metropolitan Board of Works took the opportunity while erecting the

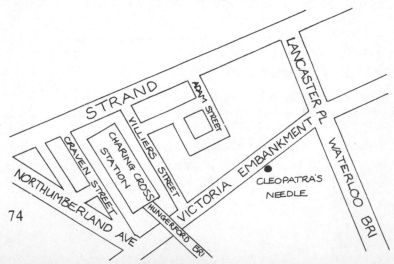

74

monument to incorporate certain carefully chosen items representing the highest achievements of the British Empire. These are contained in two large earthenware jars buried in the centre of the pedestal: a complete set of British coinage (including an Empress of India rupee) a portrait of Queen Victoria, Bradshaw's railway guide, Mappin's sculling razor, a map of London, a copy of *The Times* for the day on which the obelisk was set up, Whitaker's Almanack, a two foot rule and photographs of a dozen pretty English women. Perhaps it was felt that objects of such self-evident superiority would serve to destroy the age old curse of Cleopatra. The ancient curse, however, appears to have prevailed.

The Field of Forty Footsteps
Tavistock Square, WC1

Brothers killed in duel

Before Bloomsbury was built over at the end of the 18th century the area was known as Southampton Fields. It was a popular resort for lovers who believed that the roots of the plantain, a low growing herb which grew in these parts, was a powerful aphrodisiac. There was also a tradition among London girls that if these roots were put under their pillows at night they would dream who their future husbands would be.

Just north of the present London University buildings, behind University College, was 'the field of forty footsteps'. Here, in 1685, two brothers, soldiers in the Duke of Monmouthshire's short-lived peasant army, fought a fierce battle over a woman whom they both wished to marry. The lady in question sat by and watched. Back and forth over the field the two brothers hacked and lunged at each other until

75

eventually they both sank to the ground mortally wounded. Long after the battle, their footsteps could be seen in the ground. In each footprint the grass had withered and would never grow again. The scene of this tragedy soon became known as the Field of Forty Footsteps.

When Southampton Fields was laid out in squares and terraces, the legend of the two brothers was almost forgotten. In 1953, however, when the Indian Prime Minister visited Tavistock Square Gardens to plant a tree in honour of Ghandi, the old legend was briefly remembered. It was said that the mysterious footsteps could still be seen in the south east quarter of the gardens, near where the tree was planted. Today, it is true, one can in fact see bare patches of grass and shallow impressions in the ground just north of Nehru's tree but whether they are actually the vestiges of that fatal duel nearly 300 years ago can never be proved.

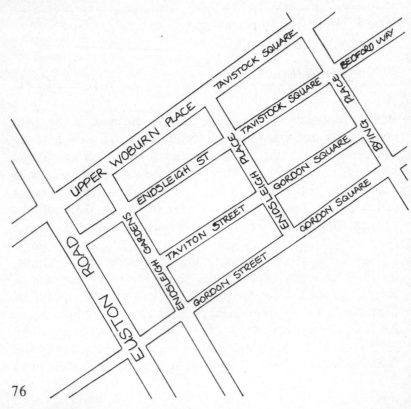

The Curse of St. Giles
St. Giles High Street, WC2

Centre Point plagued by curse of Sir John Oldcastle

Londoners have always felt a slight thrill of horror at the mention of the name 'Tyburn', the chief place of execution from about 1150 to 1759, near where Marble Arch now stands. Other execution sites were at West Smithfield, Red Lion Square, Lincoln's Inn Fields, Charing Cross and St Giles-in-the-Fields. Public executions at these sites would always attract vast crowds of spectators who would applaud or abuse the unfortunate prisoner according to his reputation. The prisoner in turn would often take the opportunity to make a final speech and his last words were often popularised in penny broadsheets. When the cart was pulled away, leaving the victim to swing by his neck, it was regarded as a sign of great bravado for the hanged man to kick his shoes into the air, and any last minute curses were considered to be extraordinarily potent. To be cursed by a hanged man was a great misfortune which only the most ardent prayer could overcome.

One of the most effective curses from the gallows was the oath sworn against the hospital of St Giles by Sir John Oldcastle in 1417 while he was hanging from the gallows which stood at the north-west end of St Giles's High Street, where Centre Point now stands. Sir John Oldcastle had led the military revolt of the lollards, followers of Wyclif, who, long before the Reformation, attacked the wealth and hypocrisy of the church. They were persecuted viciously throughout the 14th century and burnt as heretics. Sir John was a friend of Henry Prince of Wales, later Henry V, and was the original for Shakespeare's Falstaff. He was condemned to death for heresy in 1413, escaped from prison, and led the 1414 rising which failed. He became a fugitive but was captured in 1417 and died hanging in chains over a slow fire at St Giles. In the hospital standing alongside the gallows the authorities, no friends of the lollards, arranged a celebration to mark the occasion of Oldcastle's burning. Sir John, suspended in the air by iron chains around his waist, retaliated by cursing the hospital. Founded as a leper asylum in the 12th century it had long since ceased to care for the sick, and had become a comfortable home for the King's retinue. Sir John cursed it for its extreme wealth, hypocrisy, rottenness and corruption.

Sir John's curse has continued to plague St Giles ever since. During the 17th and 18th centuries, churches built on this site would decay in a surprisingly short space of time. In the 18th century St Giles Rookery was the most filthy, degraded, poverty-stricken slum in London, the scene for Hogarth's 'Gin Lane'. And even today, one wonders whether Centre Point would have stood empty for so long had it been built somewhere else.

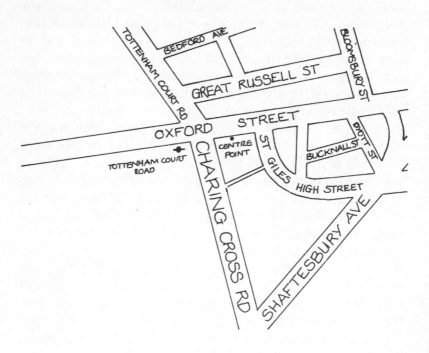

The Mysterious London Stone
Cannon Street, EC4

Legendary stone in the City

On the north side of Cannon Street, in the wall of the new Bank of China, is a curious iron grille covering a small dark opening at ground level. On peering inside one will see nothing but a piece of ordinary-looking stone—a lump of limestone without inscriptions, carvings, or markings of any kind whatever. This is London Stone, a fragment of that ancient stone so revered and wondered at by inhabitants of the City until recent times. Of all London mysteries, this is one of the most baffling.

The stone was first mentioned in a Gospel book of the west Saxons (before 940 AD). Stow, in 1598, describes the

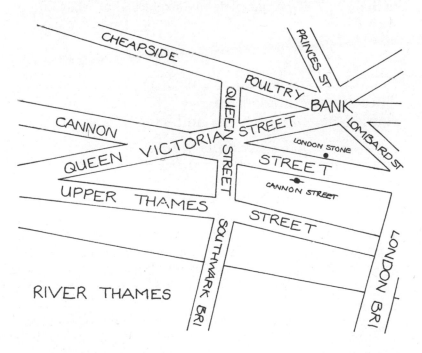

Stone 'on the south side of this High Street (i.e. Cannon Street) fixed in the ground very deep, fastened with bars of iron, and otherwise so strongly set that if carts do run against it the wheels be broken and the stone itself unshaken'.

The original function or significance of this Stone remains a mystery. In the Middle Ages proclamations would be issued from it, and solemn oaths and binding agreements sworn over it. When Jack Cade, leader of the Kentish rising of 1450, occupied London for three days, he made straight for London Stone which he ceremoniously struck with his sword.

A clue to the stone's significance is the function of other symbolic stones, such as the Coronation Stone at Westminster Abbey (referred to on page 97), and the King's Stone at Kingston-upon-Thames on which seven Anglo-Saxon kings were crowned. It is now thought that London Stone, too, was originally a symbolic source of power and authority. This would certainly explain the behaviour of Jack Cade.

The Mystery of Boadicea
Battle Bridge Road, NW1 and King's Cross Station

Is Queen Boadicea under Platform 10?

On Victoria Embankment, by Westminster Bridge, stands the statue of a woman driving a chariot of war with scythed wheels. This is a monument to the brave Queen Boadicea who led her people, the Iceni (a British tribe who inhabited what is now East Anglia), against the Imperial Roman army in 61 AD. The two girls in the chariot with her are her daughters.

Boadicea was the wife of Prasutagus, King of the Iceni, who had collaborated with the Romans at the time of their invasion of Britain under Claudius in 43 AD. He was rewarded by being allowed to continue as king, albeit under Roman administration, and his capital, Camulodunum (now Colchester), became a Roman *colonia* or settlement. When he died, the client kingdom was replaced by direct Roman rule and the wealth of the Iceni confiscated. The King's widow, Boadicea, was stripped naked and flogged and her daughters raped. Boadicea raised the standard of revolt, overran the *colonia* at Colchester and marched on the Roman city of London. The 9th Legion attempted to stop her but was defeated, and London was burnt to the ground. Suetonius Paulinus, Governor of Britain from 59 to 61, fought the Iceni with his combined force of the second, fourteenth and twentieth legions, at a site that became known as Battle Bridge (now King's Cross), and put them to flight. The Iceni population, men, women and children, were then slaughtered on such a brutal scale that Suetonius was sacked as Governor by the Emperor. Boadicea herself committed suicide, rather than face humiliation at the hands of the Romans.

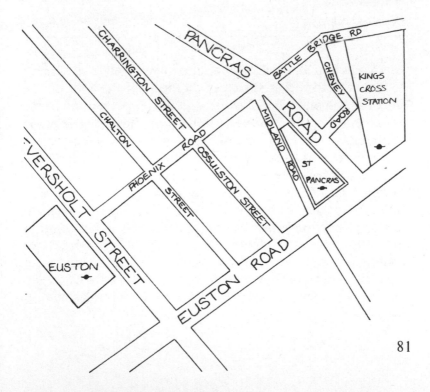

Battle Bridge Road can still be seen at King's Cross, but the site of Boadicea's grave is disputed. According to one tradition, the Queen lies buried in the ancient tumulus on the north side of Parliament Hill towards the Highgate Ponds, a spot also said to be haunted. One occasionally sees schoolboys digging here in a search for her bones, but nothing, as yet, has been found. Another tradition, supported by history books, is that Boadicea was buried at Battle Bridge and that her body now lies within the precincts of King's Cross station under the old Platform 10, now Platform 8. Until proper excavations are made the truth will never be known.

The Curse of Bow
Cheapside, EC2

Devil-worship in the City

Best known of all the City churches must surely be *St Mary-le-Bow*, Cheapside. It stands in the heart of the City on the site of a Roman Hall of Justice, and the crypt dates from the 11th century—its Norman arches, or Bows, giving the church its name. Only part of the crypt is now open, the rest being filled with corpses brought from an old churchyard. The church bells, the six 'great bells of Bow', could always be heard far and wide through the City and beyond. It was these bells that summoned Dick Whittington back to London as he made his way north up Highgate Hill. And in the 15th century the nightly 9 o'clock curfew, the hour that apprentices were expected to be within doors, was rung from this church. Even today, the definition of a Cockney, or true Londoner, is one who was born within the sound of Bow Bells.

During the Middle Ages it was believed that the church suffered from a curse due to witchcraft practised there in the 11th and 12th centuries. The church was apparently a centre for devil worshippers and Black Masses were often held under its roof. Towards the end of the 12th century the authorities made a determined effort to suppress this practice and in 1196 they caught an illicit congregation in the course of their rituals presided over by the notorious Satanist, William FitzOsbert. The devil worshippers were armed and put up a strong resistance but they were eventually smoked out. Having been drawn by the feet to the ancient gallows at the Elms, West Smithfield, they were then hanged, calling out to the end for the Devil to rescue them.

Thereafter, it appears the church was no longer used for occult practices. It was plagued, however, by an evil curse, thought to be a legacy of its use by witches. Already in 1090 there blew such a 'violent and mischievous wind' that the roof of the church was ripped off killing several people. In 1271 more people were killed when the top of the steeple fell off; and in 1284 a goldsmith who wounded a man in West Cheap sought refuge in the church only to be killed there by friends of the wounded man and hanged by the neck to give the appearance of suicide. When the truth was discovered, 16 of the murderers were executed and the defiled church interdicted by stopping up the doors and windows with thorns. In 1329 the Royal Grandstand just outside the church, from which the King would watch processions and tournaments in Cheapside, collapsed while Edward III was standing upon it, injuring several knights below. The King himself was not harmed but he was understandably furious and ordered the carpenters who built the stand to be executed. In 1666 the church was burned in the Great Fire, and rebuilt by Christopher Wren. It was destroyed yet again by bombs in the Second World War and for 20 years remained a ruin. In 1961 it was rebuilt, and as yet no further disasters have befallen it.

Coade Stone
Westminster Bridge, SE1

Lost formula for making stone

At the south side of Westminster Bridge can be seen the enormous lion which used to stand outside Waterloo station. Before that it stood on top of the Lion Brewery, Belvedere Road, South Bank, which was demolished to make room for the Festival of Britain. The lion was sculpted in 1837 out of artificial stone manufactured in the Coade Factory which also stood in Belvedere Road between 1759 and 1840.

The Stone has superb weathering qualities and was used

for outdoor monuments and ornamentation. Unfortunately, the formula for making it was kept a closely guarded secret and was lost after the closure of the factory, so that its method of manufacture remains a mystery. Other examples of Coade stone can be seen in the statues of a boy and girl over an old infants' school in the churchyard of St Botolph, Bishopsgate; the 29 vases on the parapet of Somerset House; the coats of arms on the Admiralty and at Trinity House; the caryatids at the Bank of England and the tomb of Captain Bligh of the Bounty in the churchyard of St Mary's, Lambeth.

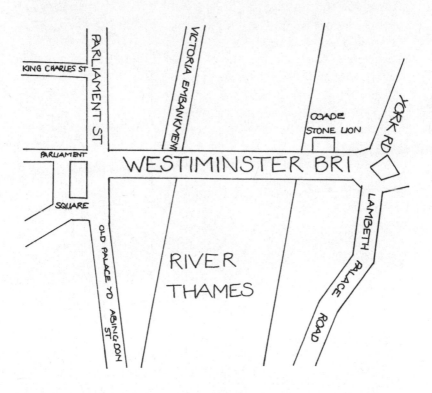

Famous Sights

London's glorious heritage has a darker side, and its best known places their secrets. Above all, the Tower—the oldest fortress prison in Europe—was the scene of crime, treachery and agonising death.

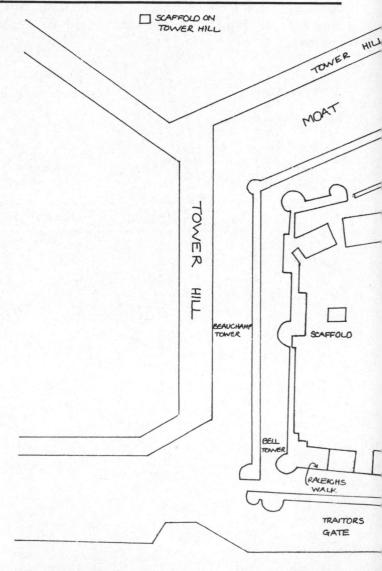

□ SCAFFOLD ON TOWER HILL

TOWER HILL

MOAT

TOWER HILL

BEAUCHAMP TOWER

SCAFFOLD

BELL TOWER

RALEIGHS WALK

TRAITORS GATE

THAMES

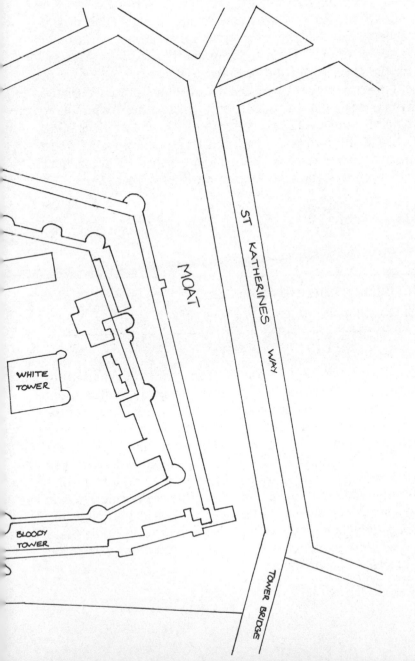

ST KATHERINES WAY

MOAT

WHITE
TOWER

BLOODY
TOWER

TOWER BRIDGE

87

The Tower of London

Tradition has it that the mortar in which the stones of the Tower were set was mixed with the blood of beasts. For hundreds of years it was the scene of royal deceit and treachery, murder and executions and the most cruel and degrading tortures. Even today when the grounds are busy with the cheerful throng of sightseers, the black history of the Tower is remembered by the ominous presence of the Ravens—symbols of death and misfortune—who have maintained their vigil here since the 13th century. It is often said that they embody the souls of victims who were executed here or who died under torture or after long incarceration in the cold, damp, rat-infested dungeons.

The Beauchamp Tower

Carvings in the walls of condemned cell

The *Beauchamp Tower* dates from the 12th and 13th centuries. In the Middle Chamber—a semi-circular room with a large window and fireplace—the name JANE can be seen cut twice in the walls (numbered 48 and 85) by Lord Guildford Dudley, husband of the unfortunate Lady Jane Gray. The assembly of names, emblems and mottos carved into these walls convey more of the misery and torture that was suffered in the Tower than any other memorial. There is also a secret passage in the Beauchamp Tower known as the Whispering Gallery where the King's spies would hide. Here they would be able to listen to the conversations carried on by unsuspecting prisoners.

Tower Green

The ghost of Anne Boleyn

Of the many hauntings at the Tower, no apparition appears so often as the headless form of Anne Boleyn, the second wife of Henry VIII, whom he secretly married in 1533. She gave birth to a daughter, the future Queen Elizabeth, in September of that year and in January 1536 she had a stillborn son. A few months later, on the 1st May, she was accused of adultery with five men, including her brother, Lord Rochford, and taken to the Tower. On the 19th May she was beheaded on *Tower Green* by an executioner brought over from St Omer. Her alleged partners in adultery were also executed, some having confessed to the crime after being tortured. Anne's ghost is usually seen coming from the Queen's House where she was imprisoned moving towards Tower Green. (The ghost has also been seen in the small upper room in *Martin Tower* where Anne was also held for a few days.)

In 1864 a guardsman of the 60th Rifles, accused of being asleep on duty, claimed that he had been keeping watch when the headless figure of a woman dressed in white emerged from a doorway of the Queen's House and glided towards him. Terrified, he passed out and was found by the captain of the guard unconscious. The court accepted the guardsman's story and he was acquitted. The headless woman has also been seen by two other guardsmen, once by the Bloody Tower and again by the Queen's House.

The White Tower

Torture in the dungeons

The Keep, known as the *White Tower*, was built by William the Conqueror in the 11th century. On the main floor is a crypt where one can see an execution block on which several cuts from the headsman's axe are still visible. Instruments of torture can also be seen including thumb screws, a spiked collar, devices for securing prisoners feet and a crushing instrument known as 'The Scavenger's Daughter' which could slowly squeeze a man to death. In the Dungeons are three chambers where the torture was carried out. Guy Fawkes (who tried to blow up the Houses of Parliament in 1605 when King James was due to make his speech from the throne) was interrogated here while being slowly torn limb from limb on the Rack. In these small rooms people often claim to sense an atmosphere of human suffering, as if the agony of the tortured had become imprinted in the very walls. Some even claim to have heard the victims' groans echoing faintly from these rooms.

In St John's Chapel, dating from the 12th century, Simon Sudbury, Archbishop of Canterbury, was put to death by rebellious peasants during the Peasants Revolt of 1381. Here too, in 1483, Sir Thomas Brackenbury received instructions from Richard III to kill his two young nephews, Edward V and his brother Richard Duke of York. The boys are said to have been suffocated in the *Bloody Tower* whilst sleeping in their beds. The bones of two young boys, thought to be the princes, were discovered in 1674, buried in a wooden box under some stairs leading to the Chapel in the White Tower. Ever since, there have been persistent reports of the ghosts of these young princes appearing by the wall where the bodies were found. They are always together, holding hands as if to comfort one another.

Raleigh's Walk

Sir Walter in the Bloody Tower

Sir Walter Raleigh knew the Tower of London well. He stayed there on three separate occasions, the longest being for 12 years from 1603 to 1615.

Raleigh entered the court of Elizabeth I as a protege of the Earl of Leicester and soon found favour with the Queen by his quick-witted flattery. He embarked on many adventures at sea, took possession of territory in America which he named Virginia in the Queen's honour, introduced the smoking of tobacco to England and helped to organise the fleet against the Spanish Armada. His downfall began in 1592 when Elizabeth became jealous and outraged at his seduction of Elizabeth Throckmorton, one of her Maids of Honour whose pregnancy brought the affair to her attention. Both were committed to the Tower for their indiscretion but were soon set free and allowed to marry.

When James I came to the throne Raleigh began to suffer from political intrigues, and in 1603 he was arrested and condemned to death as a traitor. Reprieved at the last moment, he was sent to the Tower of London and held in the *Bloody Tower* where he wrote his famous *History of the World*. The ramparts between the Bloody Tower and the Queen's House where he often used to walk are known as 'Raleigh's Walk'. In 1616 the King released him for fresh 'raiding' expeditions to the West Indies, but he returned empty-handed and was again lodged in the Tower, condemned to die under his old sentence of 1603. On October 29th, 1618, he mounted the scaffold at Old Palace Yard, Westminster, and feeling the blade of the axe he said: 'This gives me no fear. It is a sharp medicine to cure me of all my diseases'. He was buried in St Margaret's Church, Westminster.

Raleigh's ghost appears at the Tower almost as frequently as that of Anne Boleyn. He paces back and forth along

Raleigh's Walk on moonlit nights with his head carried under his arm. At the slightest movement or disturbance, however, he vanishes instantly.

The Jewel House

Weird Ghosts haunt Keeper of Crown Jewels

No-one can explain why the *Jewel House* should be haunted by the strange and unusual ghostly manifestations that have appeared there. An unnerving experience has been vividly described by Mr Edmond Lenthal Swift, Keeper of the Crown Jewels from 1814 to 1842 and on all accounts a most truthful and sober man.

'One Sunday night in October 1817, I was at supper with my wife, our little boy, and my wife's sister in the sittingroom of the Jewel House, which is said to have been the "doleful prison" of Anne Boleyn and of the ten Bishops whom Oliver Cromwell piously accommodated there. The doors were all closed, heavy and dark curtains were let down over the windows, and the only light in the room was that of two candles on the table. I sat at the foot of the table, my son on my right, my wife fronting the chimney piece, and her sister on the opposite side.

'I had offered a glass of wine and water to my wife, when on putting it to her lips she paused, and exclaimed—"Good God! What is that?" I looked up and saw a cylindrical figure, like a glass tube, something about the thickness of my arm, hovering between the ceiling and the table; its contents appeared to be a dense fluid, white and pale azure, like to the gathering of a summer cloud, and incessantly rolling and mingling within the cylinder. This lasted about two minutes, when it began slowly to move along the table before my son

92

and myself. Passing behind my wife it paused for a moment over her right shoulder. Instantly she crouched down, and shrieked out, "Oh Christ! It has seized me".

'Even now as I write I feel the horror of that moment, I caught up my chair striking at the "appearance" with a blow that hit the wainscot behind her. It then crossed the upper end of the table and disappeared in the recess of the opposite window. I rushed upstairs to the other children's room, and told the terrified nurse what I had seen. Meanwhile other domestics had hurried into the parlour where their mistress was recounting in detail what had happened. The marvel—some will say the absurdity—of all this is enhanced by the fact that neither my sister-in-law nor my son beheld the "appearance", though to their mortal vision it was as apparent as it was to my wife's and mine'.

Edmond Swift described another extraordinary ghost, from an account told to him by a sentry keeping guard at the door of the Jewel House. At about midnight the sentry was suddenly alarmed by the figure of a huge bear that emerged from the doorway. He lunged at it with his bayonet which to his horror merely passed through the shadowy form and stuck fast in the oaken door. The terrified man fainted and was found lying on the ground unconscious. Edmond Swift saw him on the following morning. He was changed beyond recognition, still trembling and frightened out of his wits. Although he managed to describe what he had seen he never recovered. Within two days he was dead.

It is not surprising that a phantom bear should appear at the Tower when one considers that a Royal Zoo was housed here for many hundreds of years. The animals would be kept in the *Lion Tower* which used to stand where guidebooks and postcards are now sold near the entrance at Middle Tower. In 1604 James I and his entire court visited the Tower to be entertained by a combat between a lion, a lioness and a live cock. The Royal Menagerie was eventually transferred to Regent's Park when the London Zoo was opened in 1835.

Treasure in the Bell Tower

'I do believe there must be money hid somewhere'.—*Pepys*

Is there hidden treasure buried in the grounds of the Tower? A solid gold crown was found during excavations to the east of the White Tower, and other treasures are still being discovered as more of the ancient building is gradually unearthed. But a valuable hoard far exceeding these may lie buried somewhere in the *Bell Tower*. It is referred to as the 'Barkstead Treasure'.

John Barkstead was a wealthy City jeweller of Cheapside whom Oliver Cromwell appointed as Lieutenant of the Tower. As was usual in those days he extracted over £50,000 from the prisoners in his custody, which today would be worth several million pounds. When the monarchy was restored in 1660 he was sentenced as a regicide to be drawn, hanged and quartered at Tyburn, but in the haste to have him executed the King forgot to ask him where he had hidden his wealth. Barkstead's former mistress later announced that the treasure was buried in the Bell Tower, and the King ordered Samuel Pepys to find it. Pepys spent many days in the cellars digging up every inch of ground but with no success.

The search was resumed quite recently with the aid of electronic detecting devices, beyond the ground already explored by Samuel Pepys. Several very promising readings were obtained but the authorities refused permission to carry out excavations because of the damage that would be caused to the buildings.

Tower Hill

'Behold the head of a traitor'

It was regarded as a privilege to be executed within the Tower since the public were not admitted. You were spared the indignity of the headsman holding your severed head aloft for all to see and announcing, 'Behold the head of a traitor'. Most prisoners, however, were executed outside the Tower, at the scaffold on *Tower Hill*.

The site of this scaffold is clearly marked to the west of the gardens. Altogether it saw the death of over 125 people between 1388 and 1747. The scaffold was about 5 feet high, made of rough planks with a railing surrounding it. The whole structure was draped in black. Sawdust was scattered over the surface to soak up any blood, and a basket stood beside the block to receive the head. Access was by means of a short wooden staircase that was apparently somewhat unsteady. Sir Thomas More, on his way to execution turned to the Lieutenant: 'See me safely up' he said, 'For my coming down I can shift for myself'.

Westminster Abbey

One of London's lost rivers, the Tyburn, used to flow into the Thames at the Isle of Thorney. This island, surrounded by Marshes, was long regarded as a sacred place. Primitive churches had stood here before Westminster Abbey was erected in the 11th century. A more promising haunt of the supernatural than this 900 year old building with such distinguished corpses beneath its stone floors would be hard to imagine.

The Haunted Abbey
Ghosts from the 14th century

The best known ghost is that of Father Benedictus, a monk who was murdered when thieves broke into the Abbey in 1303. He has often been seen walking through the cloisters in the evening between 5 and 6 o'clock, and has sometimes been heard talking to himself in a kind of 'Elizabethan' accent. He is tall and thin wearing priests' robes and a cowl under which his large head with deep set eyes, pale grey skin and prominent nose presents an awesome and sinister appearance.

In the 15th century the choir chapel by the north door was haunted by the ghost of a man who was stabbed to death in 1378. He had escaped from the Tower of London and was being pursued by 50 armed men. He sought refuge in Westminster Abbey where the Deacon was celebrating High Mass, but the armed posse pursued him, and with flagrant disregard of the holy right of sanctuary, hacked him down as he fled round the Choir. He fell dead with 12 stab wounds in front of the Prior's stall. The authorities were so horrified by this desecration of the Abbey they gave him a martyr's burial and closed the church for four months. Soon afterwards a blood-stained ghost was seen kneeling in the vicinity of the Choir with his arms raised as if to defend himself. Its appearance has not been seen since the mid 17th century, though the sound of armed men and the clash of steel has occasionally been heard near the north door.

The Coronation Stone

Mysterious stone from Scotland

In the Chapel of St Edward the Confessor stands the ancient
Coronation Chair on which almost every monarch since the
13th century has been crowned. Beneath it is a mysterious
stone, the *Stone of Scone*, brought to the Abbey in 1297 by
Edward I.

This reddish sandstone block had previously rested at
Scone in Perthshire, Scotland, where it had been used in the
coronations of 34 Scottish kings. It is said to have been the
pillow at Bethel on which Jacob dreamt of the Angels. The
Prophet Jeremiah took it with him on his travels, and a

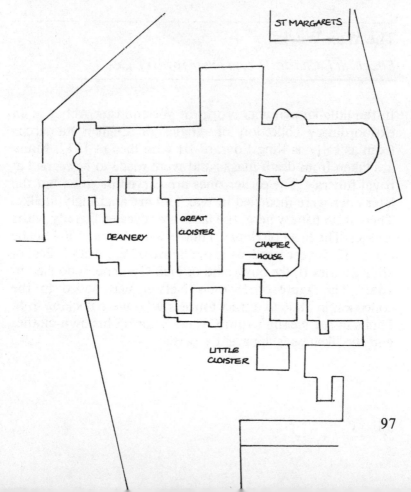

Jewish princess who married an Irish king brought it to Ireland to serve as their coronation stone. From here it was taken to Scotland in about 850 AD.

The much-travelled stone is still subjected to disturbance and upheaval from time to time. In 1940 when a German invasion was expected both the Coronation Chair and the stone were buried and the secret of their location entrusted to the Canadian Prime Minister. On Christmas Day, 1950, the Stone was seized by Scottish Nationalists and taken back to Scotland. It was retrieved in time for the coronation of Elizabeth II in 1953.

The Wax Works

Elizabeth I, Charles II, and other royal effigies

In the little-known wax works at Westminster Abbey is an extraordinary collection of effigies of English monarchs from as early as King Edward III who died in 1377. Many are taken from death masks and were made to be carried at royal funerals. The earlier ones are carved in wood but the later ones were modelled in wax and are amazingly lifelike. There is no flattery here; the faces are revealed literally warts and all. The head of Henry Tudor, who died in 1509 at the age of 52, is very good, as is the figure of Elizabeth I. Best of all is Charles II, the boyfriend of Nell Gwynne, who died in 1685. The figure of Horatio Nelson was added to the collection in 1806 to attract tourists who were flocking to St Paul's to see Nelson's tomb. He is wearing his own clothes and the likeness is apparently perfect.

Chamber of the Pyx

Robbery at the Abbey

The Crown Jewels can be seen today within the safety of the Tower of London. They were not always housed there. In the Middle Ages the King kept his valuables at Westminster, and one can still see the old *Jewel Tower* across the road from the Victoria Tower and House of Lords. An even older depository of royal treasure is the *Chamber of the Pyx* in Westminster Abbey. It can be entered from the East Walk through an enormous archway with massive double doors and seven locks and is the most impregnable dungeon in the Abbey. In spite of its strength, however, the Chamber was broken into and plundered in 1303.

Almost the entire wealth of King Edward I amounting to more than two years collection of royal taxes, was being kept in the Chamber. The King himself was away fighting in Scotland. The Abbot of Westminster and 48 monks in collusion with the Keeper of the King's Palace spent many painstaking months arranging the burglary. They were assisted by a wool merchant named Richard de Podelicote whose role was to help dispose of the valuables. A crop of hemp had been carefully grown by the monks in the churchyard surrounding the building in order to provide a cover for their operations. Eventually the crime was discovered and the King sent his men up and down the country in an effort to recover his treasure. Some was found buried in Kentish Town and some in the possession of wealthy London merchants. There were pieces as far away as Northampton and Colchester, and others hidden behind tombstones in St Margaret's churchyard, Westminster. Much was never recovered, however, and it used to be said that within the grounds of the Abbey and of St Margaret's there are pieces of the Crown Jewels still hidden.

In the late 19th century when the Chamber of the Pyx was being explored a hidden doorway was discovered at the old entrance to the Treasury. Fixed to the door were pieces of white leather which, on closer examination, were found to be human skin. As part of his terrible punishment Richard de Podelicote had been flayed alive and his skin nailed to the door as a warning to others contemplating robbery. Fragments of skin still remain under the iron clamps of the door.

Trafalgar Square

Madame du Barry's secret

Buried somewhere in the neighbourhood of *Trafalgar Square* lie the Crown Jewels of France. Madame du Barry, mistress of Louis XV, visited England in 1793 to raise money for the Counter-Revolution, bringing with her the French Crown Jewels which she had been given by the late King. While in London she stayed at a house in Pall Mall. When she returned to France she was carefully searched by the French authorities but no trace of the jewels could be found. To this day they have not been discovered. It is said that she buried them for safe-keeping when she arrived in London at a place not far from her house. Moreover, she is supposed to have paid a visit to the Royal Mews for this purpose when the Mews stood at the east end of Pall Mall. They were subsequently demolished in the 1820's to make way for Trafalgar Square and the National Gallery. Whether the Crown Jewels are still there we shall never know; Du Barry's secret died with her on the guillotine.

The nearby church of *St Martin's-in-the-Fields* is also said to contain buried treasure. It stands on the site of an older church and in the crypt you can still see an ancient parish chest made of elm and the old whipping post.

Somewhere here lies the legendary treasure, much sought after in the Middle Ages. At one time people could be seen digging for it at all times of the day and night, and even the King himself once ordered the sheriff of London to assist in the search. Although nothing was found, belief in the treasure lasted for many years.

A neighbouring church, *St Martin's-le-Grand*, which used to stand at the corner of William IV Street on the site now occupied by the post office, was so plagued by treasure hunters that in the 14th century the Dean of St Paul's publicly rebuked them for defiling a sacred building on the Sabbath.

The square today is best known for its pigeons. It is also the traditional scene of political demonstrations. For this reason, perhaps, it has an unobtrusive litte police station hidden away inside one of the large stone street lamps at the corners of the square. Inside, there is room for one policeman and a telephone in direct communication with police headquarters at Scotland Yard. You can identify it quite easily by the slits in the walls which enable the occupant to keep a watch on the square without being seen.

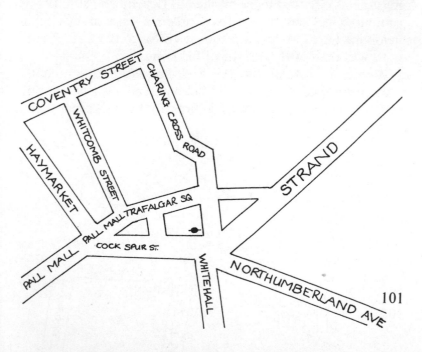

Piccadilly Circus

Scandal at the Cafe Royal

Piccadilly Circus forms the boundary between respectable St James and disreputable Soho, and it shares a bit of both. On the south and west sides are some of the most prestigious shops in London, while on the east are a jumble of rather saucy boutiques, bookshops and publishers. Below, in the Underground station and the 'cottages' you can see the 'Dilly Boys' parading themselves for the attraction of customers. They also congregate in such numbers on the pavement at the bottom of Regent Street that the place is known as the 'Meat Rack'.

This same combination of scandal and respectability can be found in many of Piccadilly's institutions. The famous *Cafe Royal*, for example, with its imposing frontage on Regent Street attended by liveried doormen in tophats and tails has a sordid little back entrance in Glasshouse Street for the use of the staff. Here a nightwatchman was shot dead in mysterious circumstances on the 6th December 1894. It was rumoured he had been mixed up in a case of blackmail involving Oscar Wilde, a frequent visitor to the Cafe Royal, who was then at the height of his fame.

A recent scandal hit the well-known and eminently respectable *RAC Club* in Pall Mall when an attractive young girl, Sarah Gibson, who was an assistant house-keeper there,

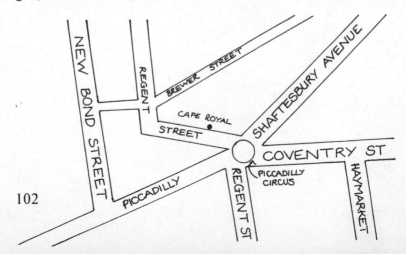

102

was found dead in her bedroom. She had been raped and
strangled with her own nightdress. The murderer was later
found at a welfare centre in Soho and is now serving life
imprisonment.

Buckingham Palace

Royal apartments underground

Buckingham Palace was built in 1705 by the Duke of
Buckingham on what had previously been a grove of
Mulberry Trees planted by King James I for the benefit of
London's silk industry. It was re-modelled by John Nash in
about 1825, but the marble arch that he designed for it was
found to be too narrow for the royal coach to pass through.
It was therefore removed to its present position at the corner
of Oxford Street and Edgware Road where the old Tyburn
gallows used to be, and is simply referred to as Marble Arch.

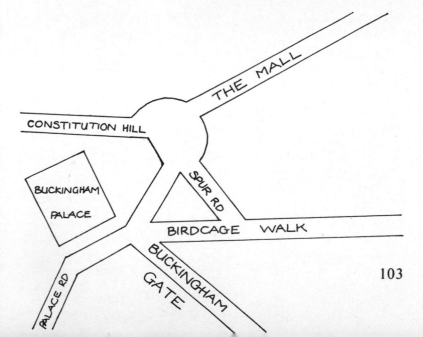

A comparatively recent addition to the Palace that is not widely known about is the underground complex of royal apartments for use in the event of nuclear war. This came to light when the new Victoria Line was being excavated between Victoria and Green Park. Instead of taking the shortest and most direct route under the Palace the engineers were obliged to make a detour at least 350 yards to the east. The royal bomb shelter is said to be linked to the network of tunnels beneath the *Citadel* at the other end of the Mall, that hulking concrete fortress built during the early years of the Second World War.

Unusual Pubs

If the visitor to London wants to see how the British really live he should try a portion of chips wrapped in greasy paper and a pint of 'bitter' at the bar of a local pub. The pubs mentioned in this guide serve the same drinks as others do but have unusual or mysterious features.

The Cheshire Cheese
Fleet Street, EC4

Dr. Johnson's favourite pub

Famous as one of Dr Johnson's favourite taverns *The Cheshire Cheese* was built soon after the Great Fire of 1666. It has a 'Dr Johnson's Corner' with a bench said to be his, and a quotation of the sort that so impressed Boswell:

No Sir! There is nothing which has yet been contrived by man, by which so much happiness has been produced as by a good tavern.

The pub is also known for its enormous pudding weighing between 50lb and 80lb and made according to a traditional recipe containing beefsteak, kidneys, oysters, larks, mushrooms and various spices. Originally it took 20 hours to cook and on a windy day could be smelt as far away as the Stock Exchange. You can sample this pudding at any time of the year.

Underneath the pub and open to visitors is a 14th century crypt from the old Whitefriars' monastery that was situated here in the Middle Ages (see page 123).

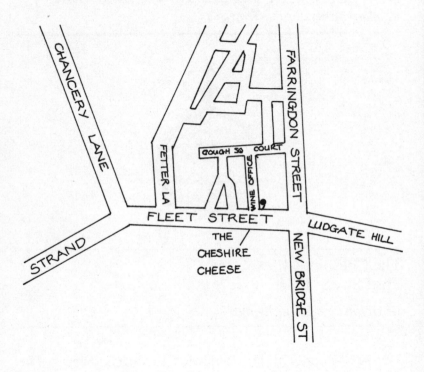

Dirty Dick's
202 Bishopsgate, EC2

Have a drink in this chamber of horrors

At Dirty Dick's you can enjoy a drink surrounded by dead cats, bones, cobwebs and other delights. Dirty Dick was in fact an 18th century dandy named Nathaniel Bentley, a wealthy man who always dressed in the height of fashion. He became engaged to a young woman with whom he was madly in love and arranged a banquet to celebrate the occasion. On the very day of the banquet, however, he received news of her death, a blow from which he never recovered. He sealed the dining room and ordered that it should never be opened again while he lived. He then led a solitary life neither washing nor changing his clothes. When he died 40 years later the dining room was at last opened. It was full of cobwebs and the skeletons of bats, mice, rats and other horrors. So unusual was this rare collection of filth that it was put up for sale and purchased by the owner of the pub where these objects can now be seen.

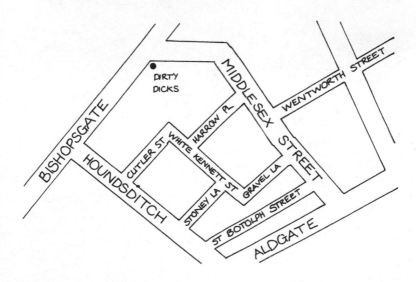

The Prospect of Whitby
Wapping Wall, E1

Famous riverside pub

Said to date from the reign of Henry VIII this riverside tavern is one of the oldest and most attractive pubs in London. It has everything: stout timbered ceilings, a massive stone fireplace and a gallery outside over-looking the river. Upstream from here one can see Execution Dock where pirates would be hanged in chains at low tide and left until three tides had swept over them. (See page 134)

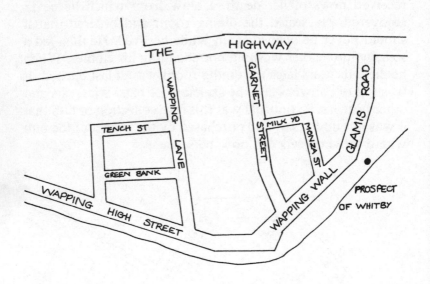

The Blind Beggar
337 Whitechapel Road, E1

Where Ronnie Kray shot George Cornell

The Blind Beggar is probably best known as the scene of the murder of George Cornell by Ronnie Kray in 1966, mentioned on page 13. It takes its name from the 'Blind Beggar of Bethnal Green' who used to beg in the Whitechapel Road at a site where the pub now stands. An old legend tells how Henry de Montfort, son of the famous Simon de Montfort, was wounded in the face at the Battle of Eavesham in 1265. Ashamed of his disfigurement he disappeared and became a beggar. His daughter, Elizabeth, grew up to be one of the most beautiful girls in London and many a suitor desired to marry her. They soon lost interest, however, when she told them who she was. In the words of the old folk song:

'My father, shee said, is soone to be seene,
The seely blind beggar of Bednall Greene,
That daily sits begging for charitie,
He is the good father of pretty Bessee'.

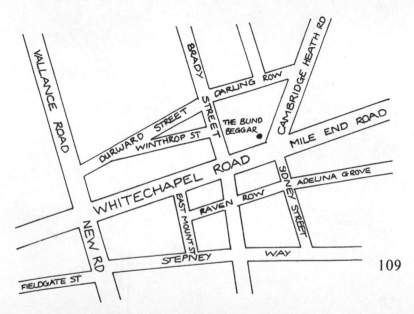

One day, so the story goes, a romantic knight whose love for Bess paid no regard to her father's occupation agreed to marry her, and at their wedding the blind beggar revealed his true identity and presented the groom with a dowry of £3,000.

The Nag's Head
324 Hackney Road, E2

Exorcists from the Daily Mirror

One of London's most haunted pubs is undoubtedly *The Nag's Head*, Bethnal Green. It is managed by Leslie and Carol Andreetti, who have lived there for about two years. When they first moved in they would hear doors banging and footsteps on the stairs at night. And the bath taps would turn on by themselves. Leslie has seen a mysterious blue mist hovering above the floor in a small top room, and Carol is constantly aware of the presence of spirits trying to possess her.

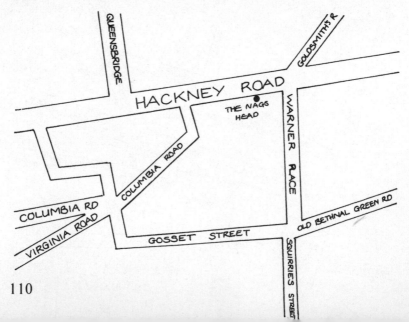

What draws the supernatural to The Nag's Head is not known, although it is said that several suicides have been committed here. About 10 years ago the *Daily Mirror* organised an attempt to exorcise the spirits, but this was unsuccessful.

The Widow's Son
75 Devons Road, Bow, E3

Was the old widow a witch?

Every Good Friday a sailor hangs a hot-cross bun in the window of *The Widow's Son*, continuing a tradition started in the late 18th century by a widow whose only son was drowned at sea. He had assured her that he would be back by Easter, and his mother refused to give up hope for his return. On Good Friday she sat waiting all day with tea and buns on the table, a ritual she repeated every Easter until she died. Over the years the cottage became known as the 'Bun House'.

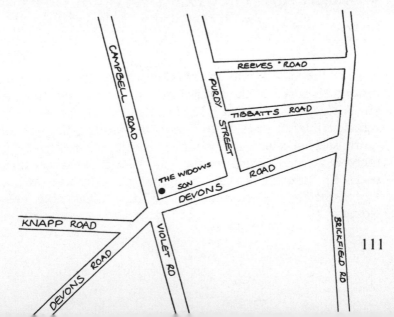

When the present pub was built on the site of the old cottage the custom continued and The Widow's Son now has over 150 hot-cross buns suspended from a beam in the bar.

Very recently the owners of the pub discovered a large old flagstone in the cellar that may well have been part of the original widow's cottage. When the earth was scraped away from its surface it was found to be divided into six squares, each square with a different number carved upon it. The mystery of this stone has yet to be solved. It may have been used for playing skittles. On the other hand it resembles those ancient Egyptian figures divided into six squares used by witches in the 16th and 17th centuries for prophesying the future. Could it be that the old widow was in fact a witch, and that the hanging up of hot-cross buns had some sinister purpose quite unconnected with the commemoration of her departed son?

The Hoop & Grapes
47 Aldgate High Street, EC3

London's oldest pub

This is the oldest pub in London dating from the 13th century. It survived the Great Fire and is now scheduled as an Ancient Monument. The leaded windows and the wooden interior date from the 17th century, though the worn sloping stairs are probably earlier. From the cellar there is a secret tunnel leading down to the Thames once used by smugglers for bringing in duty-free drink. Unfortunately the entrance to this tunnel has now been closed.

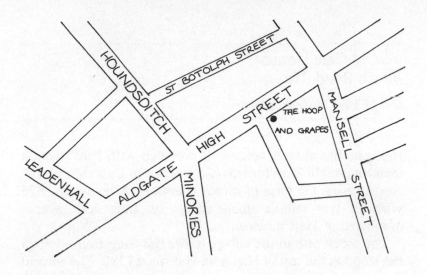

The Sherlock Holmes
10 Northumberland Street, WC2

A Sherlock Holmes museum

The Sherlock Holmes contains a reconstruction of the great detective's study at 221b Baker Street, full of documents, letters and other objects such as his pipe, deerstalker, violin, and magnifying-glass. It also has the handcuffs referred to in *A Study in Scarlet*, the airgun walking-stick that Colonel Sebastian Moran used in an attempt on Sherlock Holmes' life, and the footprints of a giant hound.

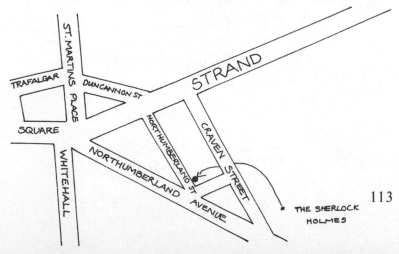

Ye Old Gate House
North Road, N6

Old Mother Marnes' ghost

Highgate has always been well provided with Inns being a main overnight stop for travellers between London and the North before the days of motor transport. Already by 1826 when it was still a small village its Inns and taverns numbered at least nineteen.

The oldest pub in the village is *The Old Gate House* which has stood at the top of Highgate Hill since 1380. The second floor used to house an ancient courtroom where magistrates seated at each end would try prisoners simultaneously. A large rambling house with winding corridors and hidden stairways, it contained a secret cupboard from which Dick Turpin, the highwayman, made one of his many escapes. The oldest part of the present building is the gallery, haunted by the ghost of Mother Marnes who was murdered and robbed here while a guest at the tavern.

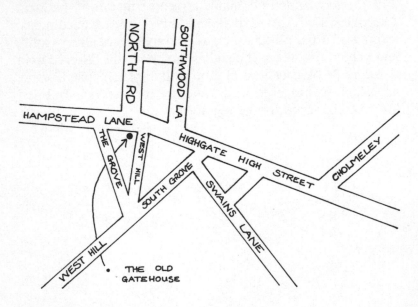

The Spaniard's Inn
Spaniard's Road, NW3

Favourite haunt of highwaymen

Built in 1630, this old coaching Inn stands opposite a former toll-gate on the edge of Hampstead Heath near Kenwood House. Dick Turpin, the highwayman, would often stay here in the 1730's, and you can see one of his pistols and a bullet he fired while robbing a coach on the road nearby. His ghost continued to haunt the neighbourhood after his death, and is still seen riding along the Spaniard's road in a black coat and three-cornered hat. A former landlord of the Inn would sometimes hear the sound of a horse galloping past at night.

The old stables have been converted into a paved garden where you can enjoy a drink on warm Summer evenings.

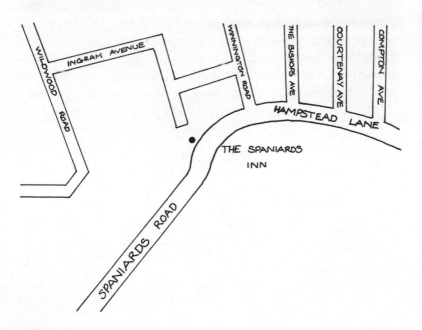

Thomas-a-Beckett
320 Old Kent Road, SE1

The boxers' pub

The Old Kent Road was the route taken by medieval pilgrims on their way from London to Canterbury to visit the grave of St Thomas-a-Beckett. They would often put up at an Inn on a site now occupied by the pub that takes his name. It is owned by Beryl Cameron-Gibbons, the only woman boxing promoter in the world, and is famous for its gymnasium used by both professional and amateur boxers. Conteh and Finnegan have trained there, as well as Henry Cooper before his retirement.

The pub is also famous for its ghosts. Beryl has often heard doors and windows opening by themselves and lights go on and off mysteriously in the beer cellar. The ghosts of three nuns have been seen on occasions walking together through the corridors on the second floor. Joe Lucy, the former British welterweight champion, saw them and even thought he heard them whispering to each other. A well-known press photographer who occasionally looks after the pub when Beryl is away was so unnerved by the eerie

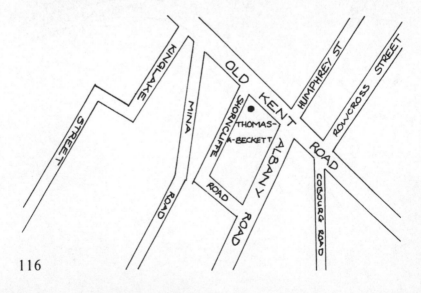

surroundings upstairs that he insists on sleeping in the bar with a loaded shotgun and his Alsatian dog.

It is interesting to note that the pub stands over an underground river, the Neckinger, which crosses under the Old Kent Road at this spot on its way to the Thames where it forms St Saviour's Dock between Shad Thames and Mill Street.

The Anchor Tap
28 Horselydown Lane, SE1

Heavy Breathing in Saloon Bar

The Anchor Tap was founded in about 1780 as a tavern for employees of the old Courage brewery nearby. They would be given tickets as part of their wages to be exchanged at the pub for free beer. This small timbered pub is haunted by a mischievous ghost referred to as 'Charlie'. He has never actually been seen but his pranks can be quite disconcerting. Objects disappear inexplicably and re-appear in the most unusual places. A watch that could not be found for many months suddenly appeared in a linen cupboard still ticking!

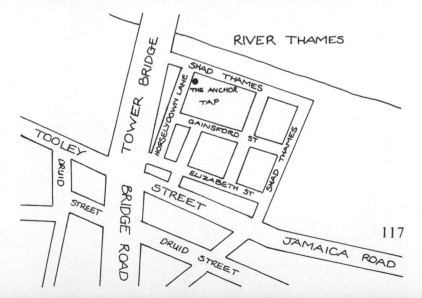

A chest of drawers was once turned upside down, and a large Irish barman who had gone into the beer cellar suddenly emerged pale and shaking having experienced an extraordinary horror he refused to describe. He would never again go down alone. Only recently the manager's wife and a barmaid were in the Saloon Bar by themselves when they both heard the sound of heavy breathing coming from the empty room. They assumed it was Charlie up to his tricks again. Who he is or why he should haunt the Anchor Tap remains a mystery. One can only say that the whole area of Horselydown Lane and Shad Thames is somewhat spooky, especially at night.

Secret Places

In the busiest centres of London there are places nobody knows—quiet secluded retreats, like the Inns of Court and Pickering Place. They are everywhere. You just have to look for them. Some of those mentioned here are more secret than others, but they should all take you—pleasantly—by surprise.

Covent Garden

Its lively past survives in hidden corners

In the 18th century Covent Garden was the city's 'West End', a licentious place frequented by actors, actresses, prostitutes and market girls. It was also a sordid and dangerous slum. No-one who cared for his safety would venture across this maze of narrow streets and alleyways after dark.

The Victorians, horrified by the poverty of these slums, abolished them by driving avenues through the worst areas: New Oxford Street, Shaftesbury Avenue, Charing Cross Road, Kingsway and the Aldwych. In spite of all the changes, however, it is still possible to capture some of the old 18th century flavour by wandering around the backstreets off Bow Street, Endell Street, Long Acre and St Martin's Lane.

Rose Street

Rose Street is an old cobbled alley between Garrick Street and Floral Street lit by a solitary gaslamp. Here in December

1679 John Dryden, the poet and playwright, was set upon by three thugs in the employment of the Earl of Rochester. The Earl believed that Dryden had written an attack on him contained in an *Essay Upon Satire*. In fact it had been written by the Earl of Mulgrave. Here, too, the notorious Edmond Curll kept his bookshop and Samuel Butler wrote his *Hudibras*.

If you turn into Rose Street today you will find a delightful little pub, *The Lamb and Flag*, containing a 17th century advertisement listing the attractions and prices of local 'jilts, prostitutes, night walkers, whores, she friends, kind women and others of the linen-lifting tribe'.

Goodwin's Court

Off St Martin's Lane are several narrow alleys and courtyards, the best of which is Goodwin's Court. You can find it by passing through the arch at 55/56 St Martin's Lane. Behind one of the beautiful 18th century shop fronts which line the sides of this court, Chippendale's furniture factory was situated between 1753 and 1813.

Bedfordbury

Goodwin's Court leads to Bedfordbury and Bedford Court, narrow backstreets surrounded by a massive Peabody Estate built rather like a prison to house the working classes.

These alleys and passageways are best seen on a dark night by the light of their dim yellow gaslamps. You might see the ghost of the actor, William Terriss, who was stabbed to death by a demented stagehand in Maiden Lane at the stage door of the Adelphi Theatre on 16th December 1896. He is a tall, well-built figure with nothing obviously ghostlike about him. Those who have seen him only notice his old-fashioned grey suit and Victorian appearance. He has also been seen at Covent Garden Underground station, Long Acre, where some of the staff became so unnerved by the haunting that they insisted on being transferred to other stations.

Adelphi Arches

South of the Strand, down Adam Street, is another 'secret place'—the immense arched vaults under the Adelphi building. Charles Dickens, who used to wander through the dark vaults when he was a boy, described them as 'a place where you might easily be murdered'.

The Arches are said to be haunted by the ghost of a young prostitute named Jenny whose body was found at the end of a tunnel called Lower Adam Street, beyond what is now an entrance to the Savoy Garage. She had been strangled and left naked under a filthy, rotting heap of decaying refuse. For many years the sound of her footsteps on the cobbled stones and her urgent cries for help have been heard echoing through the vaults late at night. Her ghostly figure has been seen lying in a corner behind some old wooden posts at the end of Lower Adam Street where her body was found; a place now called 'Jenny's hole'.

Clare Market

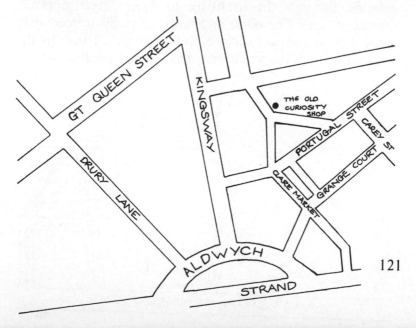

121

Of the Rookery that once occupied the neighbourhood of Clare Market little remains since the construction of Kingsway and the Aldwych in 1905. Clare Market is now just an ordinary street overwhelmed by the London School of Economics, but you can still see an ancient shop nearby, reputed to be Dickens's *Old Curiosity Shop*. And some of the older alleyways still run between Clare Market and Carey Street behind the Royal Courts of Justice in the Strand.

The Inns of Court

The old world goes on in its old ways

Lincoln's Inn and the *Temple* (Inner Temple and Middle Temple) belong to the barristers—courtroom lawyers who dress for work in wig and gown and high wing-collars. In their sedate squares and pleasant gardens a calm air of traditional learning prevails.

The full impact of the *Temple* can best be gained by entering through the archway in Fleet Street opposite Chancery Lane. The noise and bustle of traffic immediately gives way to the seclusion of Inner Temple Lane. In the space of a mere ten yards one has entered another world.

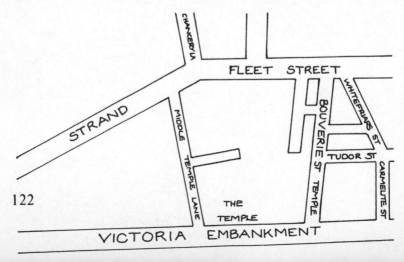

The atmosphere is accentuated at night when the whole maze of courts and arches is illuminated by the faint light of the Temple's gaslamps. It is also at night that the ghost of Sir Henry Hawkins, later Lord Brampton, is sometimes seen flitting past in wig and gown with a bundle of papers under his arm.

The gardens of the Temple used to run down to the Thames and were extended when the Victoria Embankment pushed the river back to its present course. One can still locate the old bank of the river by the position of the steps leading from Fountain Court and the south end of Essex Street.

In *Middle Temple Hall*, Middle Temple Lane, is a large oak table presented by Queen Elizabeth I, and a serving table made from Drake's ship, the *Golden Hind*. Elizabeth is said to have attended one of the performances of Shakespeare's plays that were occasionally put on here towards the end of her reign. In 1894 when the hall was being wired for electricity a secret recess was discovered in the wall near the roof containing a corpse in a remarkable state of preservation. The mystery of this recess and of the mummy's identity was never solved although examination revealed it was at least 200 years old.

Fleet Street

Dr. Johnson's territory

To the south of Fleet Street are some hidden passages around Whitefriars Street and St Bride's church. This whole area was once the site of *Whitefriars' Priory*, founded in 1241. All traces of it were thought to have disappeared after its dissolution in 1545. However, in 1883 during demolition work the north wall of 29 Bouverie Street was found to be a massive medieval structure 35 feet high with a cellar extending under Britton's Court. The cellar was being used to store coal, but it proved to be a 14th century vault. Further remains of the old monastery included a winding stone staircase leading from the Crypt to the Chapter House. The wall can still be seen inside the entrance hall of the *News of the World* building, Bouverie Street, and access to the old vault is in Britton's Court.

North of Fleet Street are dozens of little courts and alleyways, like Racquet Court with its old 18th century houses. This court was a popular place for duels, where Dennis Connel killed Thomas Wicks in 1721. The area between Wine Office Court and Red Lion Court is well known for its resident, Samuel Johnson, who lived in Bolt Court, Johnson's Court (both houses now demolished), and Gough Square where 'Dr Johnson's House' is now open as a museum.

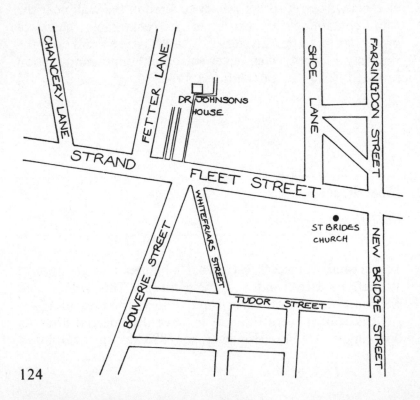

The City

Curious courtyards near St. Paul's

Wardrobe Place

Off Carter Lane is *Wardrobe Place* where the King would keep his ceremonial clothes for use on State occasions. When it burnt down in the Great Fire of 1666 its grounds were converted into the present court. On the wall of No. 1 is a small mysterious shield, the markings of which have puzzled antiquarians for many years. Below Wardrobe Place is the Church of St Andrew-by-the-Wardrobe with a bell taken from a church in Avenbury, Herefordshire. It is said that even today this bell will ring by itself whenever a vicar of Avenbury dies.

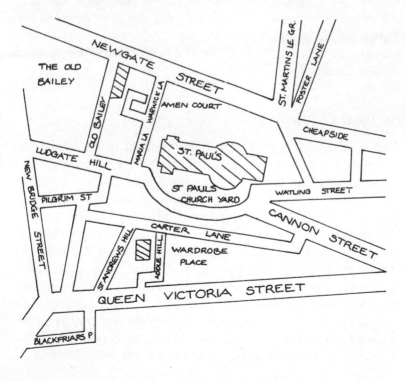

Amen Court

North of Ludgate Hill is the Old Bailey which stands on the site of the former Newgate Prison. Here public executions were held in the 19th century at the corner of Newgate Street. Behind the Old Bailey, off Warwick Lane, is *Amen Court* where you can see part of the Roman wall that used to surround the city. On the other side of this wall is 'Dead Man's Walk', a narrow passage once the graveyard of prisoners executed at Newgate.

This graveyard and the old wall in Amen Court are haunted by the ghost of Mrs Dyer, the 'baby farmer' who made a practice of strangling infant children put into her care while continuing to draw money from their parents. She would throw the corpses into the Thames, and 46 were recovered from the river after her arrest. As she passed a prison officer on her way to be hanged the old woman looked at him and said 'I will meet you again one day, sir'. He thought no more of it until, in 1902, he saw the shadowy figure of a woman in the deserted prison yard, and recognised old Mrs Dyer. Others have seen the same ghost in Amen Court.

St. Paul's Cathedral

One of the secrets of *St Paul's Cathedral* is the concealed stairway in the Bell Tower at the north west corner of the church. A hidden doorway was discovered during structural repairs to the Kitchener Memorial Chapel (formerly All Souls' Chapel) behind which a winding stairway was revealed leading up to the Cathedral dome. The doorway to these stairs has been deliberately kept secret and is difficult to detect even now. A stone door in the wall will open, however, if a hidden spring is released. The dome can also be reached by stairs from the south aisle—which *are* open to the public. These lead up to the *Whispering Gallery*, so-called because words spoken softly near the wall on one side of the gallery can be heard quite distinctly on the other side.

St. James's

The Republic of Texas in Pickering Place

St James's is dominated by exclusive Gentlemen's Clubs and expensive restaurants. But there are a few secret corners. *Pickering Place*, a little square of 18th century houses, is not indicated on most maps and is almost impossible to find unless one searches for it. The only approach is through a narrow timbered passage next to Berry Bros. at 3 St James's Street. In the passage is a plaque on the wall recording that the house at No. 3 was the official legation of the Republic of Texas when it was an independent State represented at the Court of St James's in the 1840's. Being so well hidden the square was often used for duels and was apparently the scene of the last duel ever fought in London.

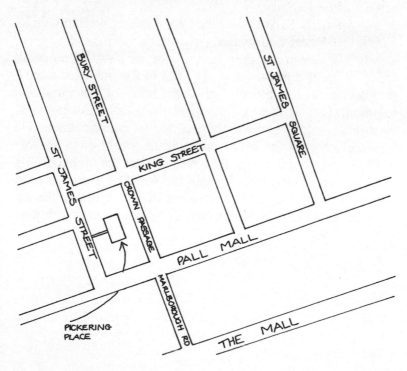

Belgravia

The Prince and the Showgirl

'Belgravia' was built by Thomas Cubitt in the 1830's as a town estate for the British aristocracy. Fortunately the massive terraces of imposing houses are relieved by delightful mews on a more human scale. You can find one behind almost every terrace, and a classic example is the mews running off Lyall Street.

Near Hyde Park Corner is *Kinnerton Street*, with its little courtyards and small old houses surprisingly close to the busy thoroughfare of Knightsbridge. Behind a door in the garden wall at the corner of Kinnerton Street and Wilton Place King Edward VII (who reigned from 1901 until his death in 1910) indulged his secret affair with the famous actress Lillie Langtry.

Old Barrack Yard and *Wilton Row* are as well hidden as Kinnerton Street and just as enchanting. Where they meet stands *The Grenadier* pub, famous for its ghost of an army officer who died in the cellar. The bar of the pub used to be a dining room for officers of the Duke of Wellington's regiment. One of these officers was once caught cheating at cards and flogged so severely that he lost consciousness. He was carried into the cellar and within a few days he was dead. Today weird noises are heard during the night coming from the cellar and occasionally the form of a man is seen climbing the stairs. The disturbances usually build up during the year to a peak in September, after which they subside.

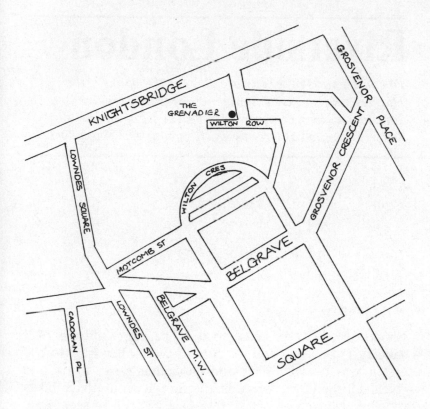

Riverside London

The oldest parts of the city are all near the banks of the Thames, and an excellent way to see historic London is to take a boat along the river, or to visit some of the old waterfronts such as Greenwich, Wapping and Southwark.

London owes its existence to the Thames. Until the 17th century Fleet Street and the Strand were often impassable, and it was quicker, safer and altogether easier to use the river. All the large houses in the Strand would have boats moored at their watergates. One gate can still be seen, now high and dry behind the Victoria Embankment Gardens, at *Watergate Walk.* It stands some hundred yards from the present course of the Thames and indicates how wide the river was before the Victoria Embankment was built in 1870.

In the 16th century as much as one quarter of London's population earned their living from the Thames, working on the boats or on the quayside. The river was also a source of great sport and entertainment. It flowed more slowly than it does today and would often freeze over. Great Ice-Fairs with booths, swings, printing-presses, and whole streets of shops would then be set up on it. In 1814, after the last Thames Fair ever to be held, a sudden thaw caused the ice to melt so quickly it floated downstream carrying all the booths and entertainments with it.

Isle of Dogs

A ghostly huntsman mourns his bride

You need transport for a visit to this 'island' isolated from the mainland by a loop in the Thames and the channels of the India and Millwall Docks.

At the southern tip lie the popular Island Gardens looking across the river to the Royal Naval College, Greenwich. From the Gardens an old foot-tunnel runs under the river to Greenwich Pier emerging by the *Cutty Sark*, last of the great tea-clippers and now open to the public.

The rest of the Isle of Dogs is a rather bleak and desolate place which has been haunted for hundreds of years by a ghostly huntsman in the sky with his phantom dogs. In the ancient forest of Hainault that used to cover the island a young nobleman celebrated his wedding by going on a wild boar hunt. His bride was unable to keep up, however, and became trapped in a marshy swamp near the river. Both she

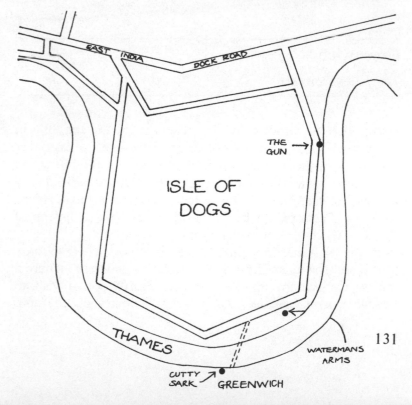

and her horse were suffocated in the quagmire. Her husband trying to find her in the forest was also engulfed by the mud. Gradually over the centuries the forest receded but the tragic hunt continues to haunt the Isle of Dogs, and gives it its name.

Then a furious blast from his ghostly horn
Is over the forest of Hainault borne
And the wild refrain of the mourners' sound
Is heard by the boatmen all night long.

There are two pubs in the Isle of Dogs worth a visit: the well-known *Waterman's Arms*, Glenaffric Avenue, which contains a mini music-hall with live entertainment on Saturday nights; and *The Gun* in Coldharbour on the east side of the island by the entrance to the docks, a traditional pub with a balcony looking out onto the river.

Greenwich

The Tulip Staircase

Greenwich is famous for its observatory on the hill in Greenwich Park where one has a good view of London over the docks to the Tower and St Paul's. Down the hill at the edge of the park is the *National Maritime Museum*, originally a royal palace. Here Anne Boleyn, second wife of Henry VIII, was arrested to be taken up river to the Tower of London where she was beheaded.

In the National Maritime Museum is the *Queen's House* renowned for its splendid hall and Tulip Staircase, where a retired clergyman, the Rev. R. W. Hardy, on a visit to England from Canada, took an extraordinary photograph.

He waited until the staircase was free from visitors and snapped it with his Zeiss Ikon 'Cortina'. When the film was processed he was amazed to see the form of a shadowy hooded figure climbing the stairs, his left hand clearly visible gripping the balustrade. The picture naturally aroused enormous interest, and was closely examined by Kodak and several photographic experts who concluded that there had been no trickery or technical interference. The ghost had not been seen before although from time to time members of the staff had reported mysterious sounds. The ghost on the photograph resembles a monk dressed in robe and cowl and may be an Abbot who once lived here.

Wapping

Shades of a violent past

Wapping High Street was once a thriving sailors' town just outside the city wall. In the 17th and 18th centuries freight from all over the world would be unloaded and seamen would spend their pay on women and drink. Packed with sailors' wives and girlfriends, innkeepers, and prostitutes, Wapping was a lively place. It was also the most violent, filthy, disease-ridden spot in England where life was 'nasty, brutish and short'. Murder was commonplace and young girls would not expect to live much beyond 25 years.

Today all this has gone. Wapping High Street is a forelorn cobbled roadway winding through bleak windowless warehouses that tower up on either side. Only at Wapping Pier Head where handsome Georgian terraces surround an ancient dock is there still some sign of life. Here, too, is a lovely old pub, *The Town of Ramsgate*, a solitary reminder of the days when Wapping High Street had over 140 taverns.

Beside *The Town of Ramsgate* a narrow alleyway leads to *Wapping Old Stairs* which still gives access to the river bank. A short distance downstream was *Execution Dock*, a gallows under Admiralty jurisdiction for crimes committed on the High Seas. The condemned man would be brought in a cart from Newgate Gaol with his executioner seated behind him. In front rode the Marshal of the Admiralty in his carriage with two City Marshals following on horseback as escort. The procession would pass along Wapping High Street and down the Old Stairs to the gallows at Execution Dock. Here the unfortunate man would be left to hang by his neck while the river washed over his body three times at high tide. Of all those who suffered this fate, best known is Captain Kidd who was convicted in 1701 for killing a seaman on his own ship by banging him over the head with a bucket. It was frequently asserted at the time that Kidd was the victim of a frame-up.

William Kidd was born in Scotland in 1645. He went to sea as a boy and made his reputation by the courage he showed in fighting the French off the coast of the American colonies. As a result he was authorised by the Governor of New York to captain a fortified gunship against the pirate ships operating in the Indian Ocean. Reports soon trickled back, however, that he had turned pirate himself. He was arrested at Boston and sent to England on a charge of piracy. It was said that his sponsors had connived at piracy in the expectation of a share in the profits. Kidd was made the fall-

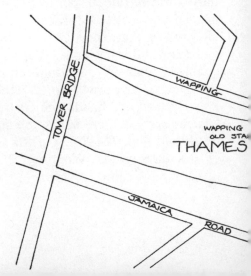

guy and hanged at Execution Dock on the 23rd May 1701 protesting his innocence to the last.

During the 18th century the ghost of Captain Kidd was often seen near Execution Dock. His pale, shadowy figure would emerge from the surface of the river and move upstream before sinking again below the water. More recently he has appeared at Wapping Old Stairs. One night after leaving The Town of Ramsgate, a local resident heard a whistling sound from the end of the alleyway that leads to the Stairs and saw the ghostly figure of an 18th century sailor coming up towards him from the river. He hastily returned to the pub and summoned his mates but when they ventured down the alleyway again the ghost had gone.

The only other pub in Wapping that still remains from the 'Good Old Days', busier than ever, is *The Prospect of Whitby* at Wapping Wall mentioned in this guide on page 108.

Under Execution Dock the famous engineer, Brunel, constructed the first tunnel ever to be driven beneath the Thames. Excavations were started in March, 1825, but the project was dogged by a series of misfortunes. It was flooded a dozen times and many lives were lost before it was finally completed in March, 1843, nearly 19 years later. Many people believed it was impossible to tunnel underneath the river, and within a few months of its opening more than a million people went to see it. Today it is still sound and dry, and is used by the Whitechapel/New Cross Underground between Wapping and Rotherhithe Stations.

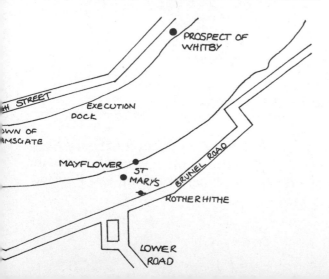

Rotherhithe

Where the Mayflower sailed for America

Across the Thames from Wapping on the south bank of the river lie Rotherhithe and Bermondsey. The old communities here, as in Wapping, were driven from the riverside in the 19th century by the erection of huge warehouses. Many streets are now bleak industrial canyons which at night provide some of the spookiest places in London. It is a brave man that will walk alone at midnight from the haunted pub *The Anchor Tap* in Horselydown Lane along Shad Thames to Jamaica Road.

In Rotherhithe Street stands the church of St Mary's where Christopher Jones lies buried. He was the master of the *Mayflower* ship which the Brownist separatists chartered to take a congregation of religious refugees to America in 1620. The ship used to be moored in the Thames at Rotherhithe near the church beside *The Mayflower* pub— one of the best riverside pubs with a veranda jutting out onto the river. The church also contains the grave of Lee Boo, prince of the Pelew Islands, who died in London in 1784. Another foreign prince who died in Rotherhithe was Mutesa II ('King Freddie') of Uganda who lived in Orchard House, Lower Road, until he died in 1969.

Southwark

The home of players and prostitutes

When London Bridge was the only bridge crossing the river, Southwark developed as an area of inns and taverns for travellers to Canterbury and all parts of south-east England.

It became a kind of medieval Soho, famous for its prostitution and entertainments.

Shakespeare's *Globe* theatre was situated here, on the south side of the present Park Street.

The first bankside theatre, the *Rose*, erected in 1587, is remembered by Rose Alley (off Park Street) and Bear Gardens (next to Rose Alley) commemorates the popular sport of bear-baiting. King James I would often amuse his friends by bringing them here to see the unfortunate bears, or bulls, being set upon by a pack of ferocious dogs.

This area is riddled with hidden corners and alleyways. From Cardinal Cap Alley, a tiny old passage off Bankside running down beside the Provost's lodgings, you get a fascinating view across the river to the west tower of St Paul's. Bankside gives a better view of St Paul's, in fact, than anywhere else in London. Christopher Wren himself used to sit here every week and watch the gradual building of his Cathedral.

Clink Street recalls the old ecclesiastical prison for heretics, the Clink, which stood within the grounds of Winchester House. From the 12th century to 1626 the house was the residence of the Bishops of Winchester. Nothing remains of it now except its courtyard, Winchester Square. The grounds of the house were known as the *Liberty of the Clink*. This became London's red light district in the Middle

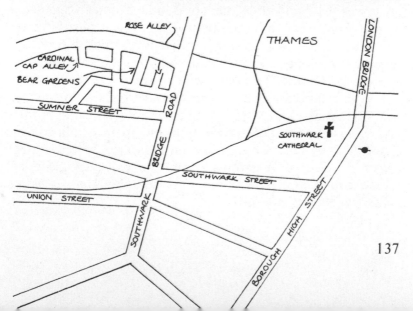

Ages and the local whores were called 'Winchester geese'. The Bishops did not object as they did very well out of the greatly increased rents that could be demanded for houses in the area! They did, however, regulate the degree of immorality within their jurisdiction by providing that 'no single woman shall take money to lie with any man except she lie with him all night till the morrow'. These women were all buried at *Cross Bones Ground*—unconsecrated ground at the junction of Union Street and Red Cross Way.

Treasure in the Thames

Spanish gold found at Lambeth

In 1842 the population of Lambeth rushed to the riverside in a mad treasure hunt after two 'water rats' in the course of their daily search for bits and pieces left by the river at low tide had found some valuable silver coins. News soon spread, and men, women and children came from far and wide and probed every inch of the bank. They unearthed a great wealth of gold and silver coins, many of them Spanish, dating from the 16th century. How much was found altogether was never known, for when the police tried to recover the money to hold an inquest on the treasure the entire population of Lambeth went 'dumb'.

People still occasionally search the riverbank at Wapping near Execution Dock where a silver casket was found in the late 19th century full of several thousand Spanish gold coins. Other fruitful sites for treasure hunters are the old fords across the river at Westminster and the Tower of London which could be crossed on foot when the Thames was shallower than it is today.

Soho

Soho

The sex business

Soho has always been rather foreign to English respectability, the home of refugees from the Continent since the late 17th century. More émigrés came to Soho after the 1848 revolutions, including the German refugee, Karl Marx, who took lodgings at the top floor of No. 28 Dean Street. Recently Gerrard Street, just south of Shaftesbury Avenue, became the focus of London's Chinese community.

A variety of businesses are carried on in Soho, the most famous being the film industry centred in Wardour Street. But the whole district is now dominated by the sex industry: strip joints, night-clubs, and prostitution.

Sex in Soho is strictly commercial. If you want to read porn there are many shops called *BOOKS* with soft porn in the front and hard porn available from the proprietor personally at the back. If you want to see nude girls you can choose between the cheap 50p strip joints dotted about Soho in their hundreds or the more expensive 'Revue' theatres offering at least some pretence of a show for about £2 a head. For so-called 'love-aids' there are several shops in Tottenham Court Road, Charing Cross Road and Cranbourn Street.

Prostitutes themselves disappeared from public view when street-walking became illegal in 1959. The girls now either operate from their flats advertising their services on notice-boards, or meet their clients as club hostesses or as

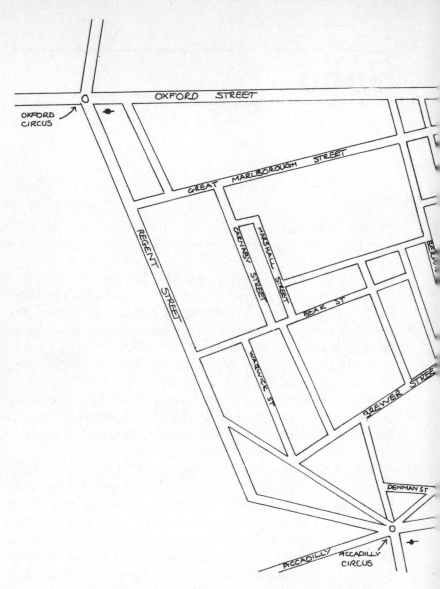

escorts for the numerous escort agencies. Newsagents'
windows in Soho contain advertisements offering the most
extraordinary goods and services for sale: a Mayfair
playpen, for instance, a large chest, or stocks and bonds
according to your taste. French lessons are offered by models
and ex-actresses, and a horde of governesses appear to be
looking for new pupils. These ads, naturally, are written in

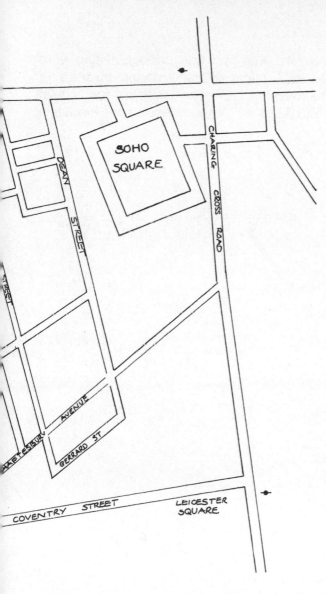

code. References to 'French lessons' for example, or to anything French refer to felatio. 'Governesses', 're-canned seats', 'stocks and bonds' or 'riding lessons' appeal to the masochist. 'Young models', or 'kittens for sale', or 'beautiful butterfly needs mounting' offer straight intercourse, while a 'young lady seeking unusual position' has an added twist. 'Costumes and props' or 'theatrical wardrobes for sale' indicates transvestism. And 'private massage', often with attractive female staff, refers to the growing business of massage-and-intercourse. A typical notice-board can be seen by the tobacconist's kiosk in Denman Street near Piccadilly Circus.

The East End

The East End

Poverty, politics and religion

The East End was originally a well-to-do City suburb, and some of its 17th century houses can still be seen in streets such as Elder Street and Wilkes Street near Spitalfields Market. A shop at 56 Artillery Lane has what must be one of the best Georgian shop fronts in London. Here the French Huguenots settled when driven out of France in 1685, and established a local silk industry which lasted until recent times.

During the 19th century London's industry moved east and with it the working population so that the East End acquired a solid working-class community frequently added to by poor immigrants from Ireland, China, India and the Jewish ghettoes of eastern Europe. The Irish settled along the waterfront in Wapping, the Chinese in Limehouse, and the Jews in Whitechapel. Driven by the starvation and poverty of Bangladesh, new immigrants are still settling in Shoreditch and Spitalfields in a Bengali community centred around Brick Lane.

Of the Chinese community in Limehouse there is very little left apart from the Chinese restaurants in Pennyfields and the West India Dock Road. The Jewish community, too, has largely moved on to the more outlying suburbs of London, although traces of Jewish life can still be found in Aldgate and Whitechapel: *Bloom's* kosher restaurant in Whitechapel High Street, famous for its salt beef; the all

night beigel shop in Vallance Road; a kosher slaughter house in Cobb Street; and the rag trade around New Road. The oldest Jewish cemetery in England, dating from the 17th century, can be found behind 253 Mile End Road. A larger Jewish cemetery founded in 1725 lies a little further up the road next to Queen Mary College. The Great Synagogue on the corner of Brick Lane and Fournier Street was originally built as a Huguenot Chapel.

The East End slums gave rise equally to politics and religion. The Salvation Army was founded by William

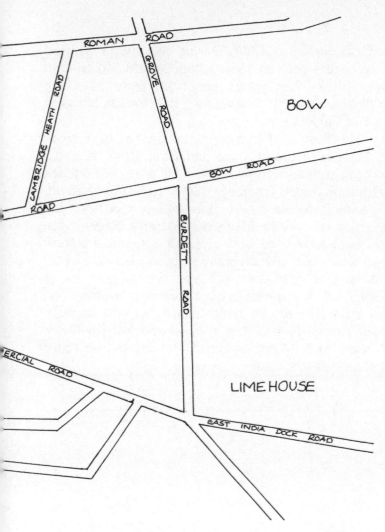

Booth in the Whitechapel Road in 1867. Like the missionaries who went to save lost souls in 'darkest Africa', William Booth led his army into what he called 'darkest England'—the festering slums of the East End. Politically, the 1880's saw a vast upsurge in working-class militancy. The girls working at *Bryant & May's* factory in Fairfield Road, Bow, (still operating today) went on strike in 1888 led by Annie Besant and Eleanor Marx-Aveling, Karl Marx's youngest daughter. Eleanor also played a leading part, alongside Ben Tillet, Tom Mann, and John Burn, in the

145

famous Dock Strike of 1889. During the 1930's political activity reached a peak in 1936 when Oswald Mosley and his fascist Black Shirts were prevented from marching through Whitechapel by thousands of East Enders blocking their path in Cable Street.

Today, the East End's main attraction are its famous markets such as Petticoat Lane and Club Row. *Petticoat Lane* is open Sundays from 9 am to 2 pm in Middlesex Street, Goulston Street, Toynbee Street and Old Castle Street, and is a general market where you can buy food, clothing and a variety of household goods. *Cheshire Street*, open Sundays, is probably the best of London's junk markets, where you can buy old furniture, clothes, books and all kinds of junk at half the price you would pay in the Portobello Road. At *Club Row*, open Sunday mornings only, you can buy all kinds of junk, as well as live animals. *Wentworth Street*, *Bethnal Green Road* and *Watney Street* markets are all general markets open all week, but are much smaller than Petticoat Lane.

Hampstead, Highgate and the Heath

The hills of Hampstead and Highgate are the highest places in London, and provide a delightful retreat from the city, particularly since they are so easily accessible by Underground.

Hampstead

Village on the Heath

By the mid 18th century, thanks to its famous well, Hampstead had been transformed from a rustic village to a well-off suburb and became 'after Scarborough and Bath and Tonbridge, one of the Politest Places in England'.

With the coming of the Underground in 1905 the village was swallowed up in the growth of London. It is still well-preserved, however, and can be seen at its best by strolling around the areas bordering Heath Street. The Hampstead poor lived in the Flask Walk and New End district where working class tenants still live today in old tenement buildings or new council flats. The old workers' cottages have mostly been tarted up and taken over by others, and the municipal Baths-and-Wash-House in Flask Walk is not as busy as it used to be.

Hampstead has its curiosities and secret places that are

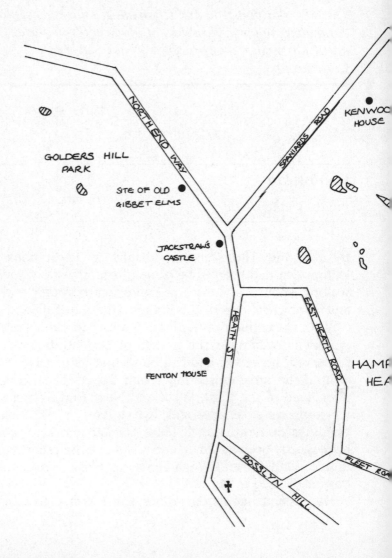

HAMPSTEAD HEATH

GOLDERS HILL
PARK

NORTH END WAY

SPANIARDS ROAD

KENWOOD
HOUSE

SITE OF OLD
GIBBET ELMS

JACKSTRAWS
CASTLE

HEATH ST

EAST HEATH ROAD

HAMP
HEA

FENTON HOUSE

ROSSLYN HILL

FLEET ROA

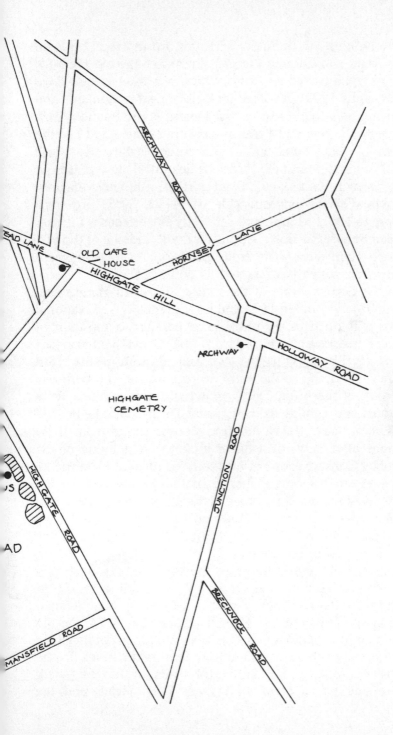

ARCHWAY ROAD

HORNSEY LANE

EAD LANE

OLD GATE HOUSE

HIGHGATE HILL

ARCHWAY

HOLLOWAY ROAD

HIGHGATE CEMETERY

JUNCTION ROAD

HIGHGATE ROAD

AD

BRECKNOCK ROAD

MANSFIELD ROAD

149

worth looking for. In Squire's Mount, for instance, between Well Road and Cannon Place, you can see the old *Lock-Up* with its small barred windows which was used as the village prison until 1832. (Another lock-up for stray donkeys and other animals found lost on the Heath, is the Pound which stands on the Heath just east of the Whitestone Pond.) At the corner of Back Lane and Heath Street is Streatley Place which leads to Mansfield Place—a delightful close of artisan cottages each with its little front garden; a hidden village of its own. On the opposite side of Heath Street are steps leading to Holly Mount, and off Holly Bush Steps is the tiny Golden Square. In Holly Mount you will find one of the best pubs in Hampstead, *The Holly Bush Inn*, a small unspoilt village pub which has retained its country flavour.

In the Grove is one of the oldest houses in Hampstead, *Fenton House*, built in 1693 and now owned by the National Trust. It is open to the public and contains a museum of musical instruments. Further up the Grove you can see *Admiral's House* built by Admiral Barton in the 18th century. He designed the house to resemble a ship with one flat roof as the Main Deck on which two cannons were mounted and another as the Quarter Deck where he hoisted the Union Jack. He would fire a royal salute from these cannons after news of a naval victory. (A painting of the house by Constable, one of his many pictures of Hampstead, hangs in the National Gallery.) In the cottage next to the house lived the novelist John Galsworthy between 1918 and 1933. Opposite Admiral's Walk on the corner of the Grove lived Du Maurier, Constable himself lived just round the corner in Lower Terrace.

Opposite Romney's house at the top of Holly Bush Hill are Mount Vernon, and Holly Walk leading down to Hampstead Parish Church past a charming little Roman Catholic church built for French refugees in 1814. On the other side of Frognal is Oak Hill Way, a hidden country lane running past a modern estate into Redington Road. In the opposite direction, Windmill Hill leads to Judges' Walk where one has a good view over West Heath and the northern suburbs of Golders Green and Hendon. There used to be a pond in the hollow below Judges' Walk and you can still see the source of the Tyburn river which now flows underground to Westminster.

The south end of Hampstead around Downshire Hill and Willow Road is also worth a visit for John Keats' house which has been opened to the public as a museum in Keat's Grove. Here, too, in South Hill Park, is *The Magdala* pub where Ruth Ellis shot her boyfriend on the pavement outside in 1955. She was the last woman in England to hang.

The Heath

London's wild open countryside

The old Heath was subject to public grazing rights for many hundreds of years but was half the size it is today. The older parts are easily recognisable by their wild uncultivated scenery, while the recent additions, Golders Hill Park, the Heath Extension, the grounds of Kenwood, and Parliament Hill, are more civilised.

In the days before the Reformation many hidden *Shrines in the Wood* could be found on the Heath. The remains of one such shrine were discovered in 1892 by young children playing with their buckets and spades on Parliament Hill Fields. A small boy digging under a hedge with his wooden spade struck a solid piece of metal which when cleaned turned out to be a silver 'Pilgrim's Flask'. After further excavations a valuable collection of religious items were uncovered including a chalice and two large silver candlesticks of ancient design.

It is a cherished belief of many local children that there are

151

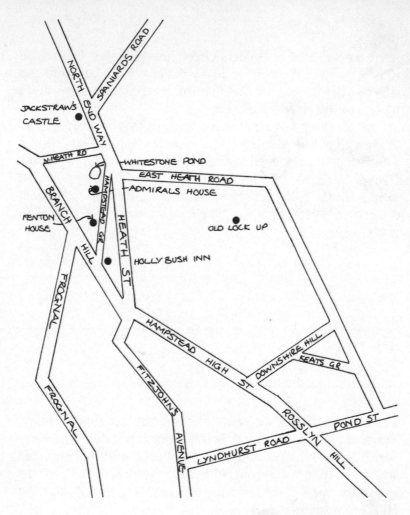

still enchanted places on the Heath, where with luck the 'little people' can be encountered. One is the clump of Fir trees standing on a small hill near the ancient burial tumulus referred to on page 82. The others are near *The Old Bull & Bush* pub at North End; one in Wild Wood near the end of Wild Wood Grove, the other just behind the houses opposite the pub near Sandy Road which crosses the Heath from Platt's Lane.

Along the main roads cutting through the Heath are Hampstead's three most famous pubs: *Jack Straw's Castle* at the top of the hill; *The Old Bull and Bush* at North End on the road to Golder's Green; and *The Spaniard's* on the road to Highgate near Kenwood. All were much frequented by highwaymen during the 17th and 18th centuries. Dick Turpin often used The Spaniard's where you can still see the room in which he slept and the place where his horse, Black Bess, was lodged. Other famous highwaymen also 'padded' these roads, including Claude Duval, Tom King, and 'Sixteen String Jack'. Platt's Lane was once called Duval's Lane after the dashing French robber who came to England in 1660 at the age of 17. For nearly ten years he terrorised the roads into London before being hanged at Tyburn. But he was the model highwayman, handsome, brave and courteous to women. Having robbed the coach at pistol-point he would invite the ladies present to dance a minuet in the moonlight. His funeral in Covent Garden church in 1670 was attended by many respectable members of Society— 'whereof most were of the beautiful sex'.

Four years after Duval's death there was a famous battle on Hampstead Heath when local citizens, armed and on horseback, pursued five highwaymen led by the notorious Francis Jackson. They were finally caught after a fierce gun-fight in which three of the pursuers and two of the robbers were killed. The highwaymen were convicted and Jackson was ordered to be 'hanged at Hampstead and gibbetted for future example'. The execution was carried out at the *Gibbet Elms*, two large trees standing on the verge of the Heath beside the road to North End just north of Jack Straw's Castle. Travellers would see his shrivelled corpse hanging in chains between the two Elms for many years afterwards.

According to tradition a secret tunnel runs underground from Highgate to the Spaniard's Inn and from there to Jack Straw's Castle. It is large enough in places for a man to ride on horseback. There are also records of underground tunnels leading from *Kenwood House*, and it has been suggested that they were used by the thieves who have stolen valuable paintings from the House on several occasions recently in spite of massive security precautions. The building is covered with burglar alarms but someone forgot to wire up the tunnels.

Highgate Cemetery

Body-snatchers raid the catacombs

On either side of Swain's Lane lies the famous Highgate cemetery, known throughout the world for the grave of *Karl Marx*, buried there in 1883. With him lie his wife, their maid Helena, and their grandson, Harry Longuet. (Engels was cremated and his ashes scattered in the English Channel near Eastbourne.)

The oldest part of the cemetery lies on the west side of ·Swain's Lane below St Michael's Church. It is by far the spookiest place in London, the haunt of ghosts and vampires and the home of several witchcraft cults. The old catacombs are fast decaying but this merely adds to the sense of death and decomposition. Several tombs have been broken into recently and the bodies removed for use in occult rituals. Not long ago a local resident opened his parked car to find an exhumed corpse in the driving seat. And in 1969 a man was arrested here late one night carrying a stake and crucifix to tackle the Highgate vampire! The ghost of an old woman has often been seen darting among the tombs, her long hair blowing in the wind. She is said to be looking for the bodies of children buried there whom she murdered.

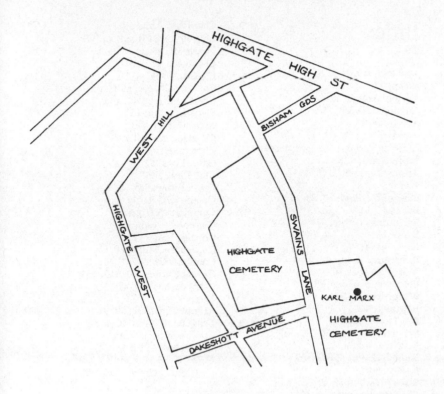

Index

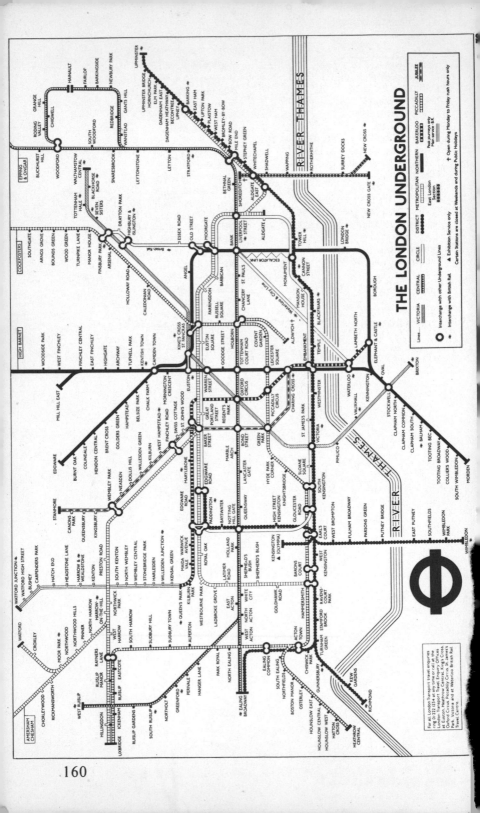

THE LONDON UNDERGROUND